PUB WALKS

—— IN ——

The Mendips

Peter Forrester

COUNTRYSIDE BOOKS
NEWBURY BERKSHIRE

First published 2004
© Peter Forrester 2004

COUNTRYSIDE BOOKS
3 Catherine Road
Newbury, Berkshire

To view our complete range of books,
please visit us at
www.countrysidebooks.co.uk

ISBN 1 85306 849 7

Maps and photographs by the author
Cover picture of Compton Bishop supplied by Bill Meadows

Produced through MRM Associates Ltd., Reading
Printed by J. W. Arrowsmith Ltd., Bristol

Contents

Introduction   6

Walk

  1   Hutton: The Old Inn *(8 miles)*   8

  2   Webbington: The Webbington Hotel *(6 miles)*   13

  3   Cheddar: The Riverside Inn *(3 miles)*   18

  4   Shipham: The Penscot Inn *(7½ miles)*   22

  5   Burrington Combe: The Burrington Inn *(7 miles)*   27

  6   Blagdon: The New Inn *(8 miles)*   31

  7   Draycott: The Strawberry Special *(3½ miles)*   35

  8   Priddy: The Queen Victoria Inn *(3 or 6 miles)*   39

  9   Wookey Hole: The Wookey Hole Inn *(3 miles)*   43

10   Wells: The Kings Head *(4 miles)*   47

11   Nr East Harptree:
      The Castle of Comfort Inn *(6 miles)*   51

12   East Harptree: The Waldegrave Arms *(6½ miles)*   55

13   Litton: The Kings Arms *(6½ miles)*   60

14   Gurney Slade: The George Inn *(4 miles)*   65

15   Stratton on the Fosse: The Kings Arms *(6 miles)*   69

AREA MAP SHOWING THE LOCATIONS OF THE WALKS

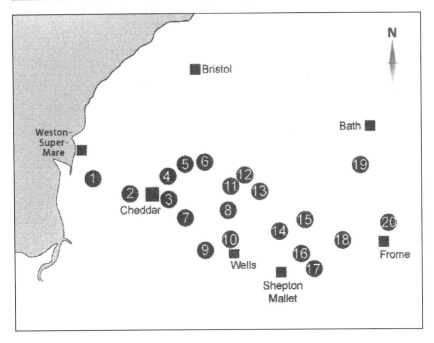

PUBLISHER'S NOTE
We hope that you obtain considerable enjoyment from this book; great care has been taken in its preparation. However, changes of landlord and actual closures are sadly not uncommon. Likewise, although at the time of publication all routes followed public rights of way or permitted paths, diversion orders can be made and permissions withdrawn.

We cannot, of course, be held responsible for such diversion orders and any inaccuracies in the text which result from these or any other changes to the routes nor any damage which might result from walkers trespassing on private property. We are anxious though that all details covering the walks are kept up to date and would therefore welcome information from readers which would be relevant to future editions.

The simple sketch maps that accompany the walks in this book are based on notes made by the author whilst checking out the routes on the ground. They are designed to show you how to reach the start and to point out the main features of the overall circuit; they contain a progression of numbers that relate to the paragraphs of the text. However, for those who like the benefit of a proper map, we recommend that you purchase the relevant Ordnance Survey sheet in the Explorer series.

16 Stoke St Michael: The Knatchbull Arms *(5 miles)* 74

17 Cranmore: The Strode Arms *(6½ miles)* 78

18 Mells: The Talbot Inn *(7½ miles)* 83

19 Wellow: The Fox and Badger *(6 miles)* 88

20 Oldford: The Ship *(4 miles)* 93

ACKNOWLEDGEMENTS

I must thank my 'man o' Mendip', PJ. No one knows his real name; it's just PJ. Many times in the White Horse Inn at Yeovil have we discussed my walks over a pint or two – he was always ready and willing to give me inside local information on all of the pubs that I have included in my book.

I also acknowledge the help given to me by the Bristol Waterworks Company. I have drawn on their report by R.G. Williams regarding water facts and particularly the technical information for Harptree Combe (Walk 12).

A special mention must also go to a book called *Somerset v Hitler*, written by Donald Brown, and published by Countryside Books. It gave me a valuable insight into the work carried out on the Mendips to help defend the area against enemy attack during the Second World War and enriched my understanding and enjoyment of several of the places I visited whilst researching the walks for this book.

INTRODUCTION

These twenty pub walks are designed to ensure that you obtain the maximum pleasure from two of our country's greatest assets – the open countryside and the local pub.

Set in the north of Somerset and arguably the jewel in the crown of this county are the Mendip Hills. Primarily formed in limestone, they range from the small village of Hutton, which lies between the town of Weston-Super-Mare and the M5 motorway, across to the town of Frome in the south-east. These hills are about 25 miles in length and about 5 miles in width. The whole area is renowned for its numerous caves, particularly those found at Wookey Hole and Cheddar. These have produced evidence of early occupation by man and there are several examples to be found on some of the walks. You will also find ruins of Roman lead mines in these hills and Walks 6 and 11 take you through the remains of old mines. The main Fosse Way, a Roman road, can be seen and experienced in Walks 15 and 17. There are also the remains of a Roman amphitheatre, perhaps the site of grisly executions in Romano British times. This is near Charterhouse but located not far from the Roman fort (Walk 6).

What is so crucial about limestone is that when in contact with water over a long period of time – and the Mendips are in contact with a lot of water – the carbon content will eventually dissolve out of the rocks, leaving huge empty spaces; hence these hills are famous for their caves and caverns.

Despite a high annual rainfall, particularly at the higher elevations, a reliable supply for those living on the Mendips plateau was always a tremendous problem. This accounts for the lack of large villages or towns upon the plateau and also explains the cluster of towns such as Wells, Cheddar, Blagdon and others dotted around the bottom of the Mendips. The foothills have always had a good and constant supply of water from the springs surrounding the hills, even during periods of extreme drought.

It is also water collection from the Mendips that was instrumental in helping to reduce the large-scale mining and quarrying that existed in this area for centuries. The demands of washing lead and silver ore and the results of quarrying often led to terrible pollution. This caused the mines and smaller quarries to be gradually closed down as the cost to stop the pollution occurring exceeded the value of what was mined or quarried. As the smaller quarries were discontinued, the damage being done to the subterranean caving system by the constant excavations ceased. Despite this there are still some major operational quarries within the Mendips. Walks 14 and 18 skirt around two of these large quarries and give you some realtime experience of their size.

The dryness of the land caused by the porous rocks has added a fantastic bonus for walkers. The ground of the Mendips is usually firm and hard with very little mud, making walking that much easier. This means that these routes are accessible at all times of the year, no matter how much rain has fallen.

Most of the Mendips Hills area is designated an Area of Outstanding Natural Beauty, and combined with the recognition of Sites of Special Scientific Interest this ensures that the region is being kept in trust for the sightseer. The visitor finds a beautiful and matchless landscape that will be spared the blemishes of modern buildings and enterprises, hopefully for ever. It is impossible for the walker to get bored on the Mendips. Every rise, valley or wood offers a surprise, whether it is the sudden appearance of a swallet or cave, or the unforgettable sight of a river disappearing from view into the rocks. The area has something for everyone and draws people from all over the world.

In this book I have tried to cover all of the Mendips so as to give an overall taste and experience of the uniqueness and mystery of the area. The routes are mostly circular or panhandled in shape and range from 3 to 8 miles, giving walkers of all abilities the chance to stretch their legs according to how they feel. Some of the walks can be shortened and this is stated where relevant. Each walk also has a simple sketch map to show the way and give a not-to-scale impression of the route.

All the pubs and inns serve food (with the exception of Walk 16, but there is a superb restaurant literally within a stone's throw from the featured pub). I have shown the telephone number and the website address where applicable, enabling you to check opening hours and book ahead for a meal if necessary. The pub car parks are also mentioned where available, but please always ask permission to park before you go for your walk (it goes without saying that you should also be a customer). Should the car park be full and you have to leave your car in the town or village, please be considerate to the needs of the local population.

I hope you enjoy these walks and have as much fun on them as I did when putting them together.

Peter Forrester

HUTTON
The Old Inn

This longer circular route encompasses the far western part of the Mendips. Starting at the picturesque village of Hutton, it moves gently up and over the hills and onto the escarpment. At Hellenge Hill a spectacular view awaits, taking in the whole stunning vista of the Somerset Levels, the Bristol Channel, Brent Knoll Hill and Steep Holm Island all in one glance. The walk then drops down into the village of Bleadon and crosses the River Axe at the flood defences. An easy stroll through the Somerset Levels along the line of the river follows before the walker doubles back to the crest of the Mendips once more, finally descending through the very pretty Canada Combe to return to the inn.

The Old Inn at Hutton has been there for some while, but time has dimmed its past history. All that can be remembered is that at the beginning of the 20th century it was burnt down and completely rebuilt. During the Second World War it formed an association with members of the airforce from what was once the nearby operational airfield at RAF Locking. Photographs of officers and men in their wartime uniforms are still on display in the bar, together with the names of those in the pictures. This 1940s' 'feel' is maintained with written mottos such as 'Kissing don't last, but cooking do!' decorating the walls. On the day I was there five real ales were on offer plus other bitters and a variety of lagers. The inn has an excellent reputation for food, with dishes ranging from rump steak topped with Stilton through to Thai red vegetable curry and going down to basic sausages and mash. Meals can be taken either in the bar, the set aside dining area or outside on the raised decking platform that fronts the road. This is a very popular pub and it is always advisable to book if you intend to have a full meal. Telephone: 01934 812336. Dogs are welcome in the bar but not in the food areas.

- **HOW TO GET THERE:** From the A38 north of Bridgwater, turn onto the A370 near the village of East Brent. At the large roundabout on the outskirts of Weston-Super-Mare, bear right onto the road through Oldmixon and continue to Hutton. The Old Inn is located on the left as you enter the village.
- **PARKING:** There is ample parking at the inn.
- **LENGTH OF THE WALK:** 8 miles. Map: OS Explorer 153 Weston-Super-Mare and Bleadon Hill (GR 351588).

THE WALK

1. Leave the inn and turn left. Walk along to the school, noting the war memorial on your right. This is unusual in that it bears homage to civilians killed as a direct result of enemy action at Oldmixon. Turn right into Church Lane. Follow the metalled path round, keeping the church on your left. On your right you will note the walled parish pound (now a private garden) – at one time almost every Mendip village maintained its own pound to hold stray animals. Immediately to the left of this, note the footpath sign. Go over the stile and walk across the field. On the day that I did this walk my attention was drawn to the calling of buzzards as they took advantage of the sea breeze from Weston-Super-Mare to climb to their hunting heights.

At the end of the field go over the stile and just before the hardcore track turn left and walk up the well-marked path through the wood. This is typical old English woodland, with a mixture of ash, oak and hazel trees. After you leave the wood the footpath meets another, crossing from right to left. Turn right and into the field, keeping the old barn on your left. Where the hedge ends, walk diagonally across the field slightly

9

to your left, heading for the point where the trees end. On the right there is an underground reservoir standing just proud of the land. At the trees go left over the stile and down the track to the road.

2. Turn right. A memorial seat to farmer George Wall has been placed at this point. You can sit here on Hellenge Hill and admire the breathtaking views that stretch before you. Ahead of you is Brent Knoll Hill, with the River Axe below, running to the sea at Uphill. To your right you can clearly see the Bristol Channel and the island of Steep Holm. Walk on down the road for about 100 yards to where the wood on your right commences. On your left, by the aptly named Wood House, go left over a stile and into a field. Follow the path down. Just before you cross over into a leafy lane, you will notice a stone-filled swallet on your left. (A swallet is a place where water from a surface stream sinks underground.) The track then leads out onto a metalled road and down to a T-junction with a stone-built wall ahead of you.

3. At this road, turn left and walk down into the village of Bleadon. The Queens Arms pub will be on your right. At the junction go straight over, keeping the church and the charming post office on your left. At the village hall and playground turn left and go into Bridge Street. Walk on down to the busy A370, keeping the shallow dyke on your right. The water is extremely clear here and I saw a small river pike basking in the sunlight.

4. At the main road turn left and pass the River Axe floodgate. Barges quite regularly navigated the river beyond this point but the installation of floodgates in 1802 stopped this. Little ports, such as Rackley, that were unfortunately located further upstream were forced to close.

Just past the river, turn left at the footpath and follow it along, keeping the river on the left. Cross over the metalwork bridge and turn right, now keeping the river on your right. In the third field, turn left and head towards the hedge to the right of the Dutch barn. At the barn, turn right and follow the footpath along for some way until you come to a group of three farms. Keep the first two farms on your left. Just past the pond full of bulrushes and immediately before the third farm building, turn left over the stile and angle across the field, keeping another farm, which comes into view, on your right.

5. Cross over the metalled road and walk straight ahead up the lane with

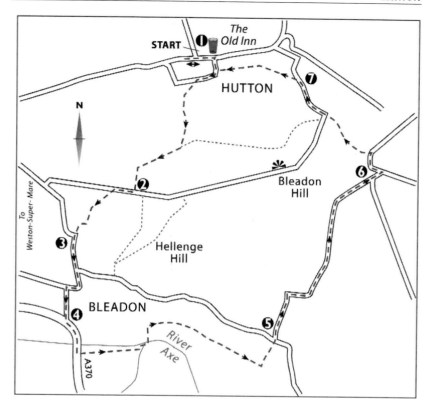

the dead-end sign. Where the metalled road runs out there is a large house on your left. The path becomes a bridleway and a notice tells you that you are now moving into a Farming and Wildlife Advisory Group area (FWAG) whose aim is to plant areas to attract wildlife. As I moved up through this area on my summer's walk I was stalked by a flight of harmless but weird looking large blue dragonflies; no doubt they were not too happy about having their sunbathing interrupted. Continue over the hill, and where the wood ends cross diagonally right over the field and along the bridleway. As you walk across this field Weston-Super-Mare and the sea are over to your left.

6. The bridleway then crosses over into a farm track. Follow this track downhill, ignoring the track joining from the right. At the next T-junction, signposted 'Bleadon', turn left and walk on downhill. After a short while the track forks left to Bleadon. Ignore this, but continue down to the farmstead just below you. Pass left through the kissing gate and into the lane. As I walked down the lane with the overgrown wooded side on my left, I was conscious of the sweet and refreshing smell of wild spearmint. Slightly further on down the lane is the tiny hamlet of Upper Canada. At the T-junction, turn right. Here the walker passes through a miniature version of Burrington Combe (see Walk 5) but with no caves. High and steeply wooded rocky valley sides welcome you to the small but pretty place known as Canada Combe.

7. After about 300 yards the combe ends. Turn left by the small pond and cross over the stile into the field. Follow the footpath along, heading towards the church and the island of Steep Holm in front of you. This footpath leads back into Church Lane. Turn right to return to the Old Inn.

WEBBINGTON
The Webbington Hotel

❦

This unusual route allows the walker a far-reaching view over the Somerset Levels and the nearby Bristol Channel, on a clear day extending south-west to Exmoor. Starting from the famous Webbington Hotel, the walker moves uphill with an outstanding vista extending to the rear. The walk follows the ridgeline along beautiful Wavering Down, with the charming village of Compton Bishop nestling in the horseshoe-shaped valley below. The route then descends into an extremely old forest known as King's Wood, giving an opportunity (perhaps) to sight what local legend has named 'the famous beast of Cross'. After Cross itself, there is the delight of walking along a riverside in the Somerset Levels and then through the Roman port of Rackley before returning to the hotel.

The Webbington Hotel is a comparatively new establishment, having been converted from a spacious family house into a country club in the 1960s. It has an unrivalled location in the area and a stunning outlook.

There is a delightful bar that welcomes walkers, with a range of lagers and beers available. Draught Guinness is also on tap. Dogs are allowed in the bar too.

During the day the hotel runs a snack bar menu only, offering among other things freshly made baguettes with local Cheddar cheese and filled jacket potatoes. An excellent range of food is available from early in the evening. Telephone: 01934 750100.

- **HOW TO GET THERE:** Turn off the A38 at the village of Cross, north of Bridgwater, onto a minor road leading westwards. Continue for about 2 miles into Webbington. The hotel is on your right.
- **PARKING:** There is parking at the hotel.
- **LENGTH OF WALK:** 6 miles. Map: OS Explorer 153 Weston-Super- Mare and Bleadon Hill (GR 382556).

THE WALK

1. Come out of the main reception area of the hotel into the car park. Turn right, with the prominent 'Webbington Hotel' sign on your right. Walk on up to the metalled track next to the vehicle garage, turning left. Go down the track to the road junction, noting the interesting white panelled house called 'The Lodge' on your right. The busy M5 motorway is clearly seen and heard on your left. Follow the lane on and up to the mobile telephone masts on your left.

2. At this point, turn right and follow the bridleway through the gateway. Ignore the track going straight up to the left. Follow the well-marked track along, and then bear sharp left uphill, ignoring the footpath that leads off to the right. A sign points the way towards Shute Shelve. As you walk up the hill, pause every so often to look at the scene that develops behind you. On reaching the crest you may come across local flying enthusiasts and their model planes, a favourite spot for them. At the top of the hill you will come to a limestone wall. Bear left here.

You can bear right if you want to and take a small detour to Crook Peak, some 400 yards away to your right. You will be getting a better view later, but if you wish to do this you should allow an additional ½ hour for your walk.

At the limestone wall, keep it on your left at all times and follow the signposted bridleway pointing towards Shute Shelve. The track is wide and spacious with local wildlife abounding. At this point the village of Compton Bishop unfolds peacefully beneath you and down to your

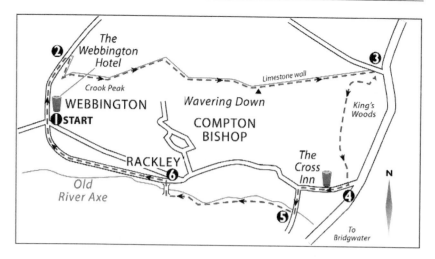

right. If ever the description of 'nestling in the valley' applies to a village, this is it. It is hard to imagine it, but during the Second World War the local school and schoolhouse were blown to bits as the result of an enemy bombing raid.

Keep the wall on your left at all times, and eventually you will reap your reward. Just as you reach the top of Wavering Down you will find a large limestone seat, chiselled into which is the inscription 'Only a hill – but all of life to me', together with '1937-2000 HBP'. Someone obviously had a great love for this place during his or her lifetime. Pause on this seat and drink in the vista that unfolds before you. On a bright day, Brent Knoll, the Bristol Channel, Wales and Exmoor can clearly be seen. The Somerset Levels also spread before you, with the River Axe beyond Compton Bishop. After a pause, walk on alongside the wall. As you approach the white trig point on your right, you will be amazed by the beautifully sudden appearance of the Cheddar Reservoir off to your right.

Wavering Down now starts to fall behind you as you walk on downhill, passing Hill Farm on the left-hand side. Just before the farm, on a large beech tree amongst a clump of others, you will find the unusually shaped and inedible fungus called dryad's saddle growing unhindered. This can grow up to 20 inches across and can add quite a bit of weight to a rotting tree, helping to pull it to one side and then eventually contributing to its downfall.

Walk on down the hill and enter King's Wood. This consists of sweet chestnuts, oaks, ash, hazel trees and pollarded small-leaved limes. The floor is quite clear of undergrowth and walking is a delight. Go down as

15

The unusual-shaped and inedible fungus called dryads saddle

far as you can and you will come to a car park, where a National Trust noticeboard tells you about the wood and its boundaries in detail.

3. Turn right here along the well-made path, keeping the field on your left. I decided to rest at this point and have a drink of water, quietly observing things around me. As I did, so something greyish in colour, fast and large, shot across my path at the periphery of my vision and disappeared into a hole to my right. Unfortunately it was far too swift for identification, but it certainly was not a fox or hare as it was far too big for either. For a moment I wondered if it were a dog? My curiosity finally got the better of me, so I walked cautiously forward. There opposite a pollarded lime tree on my left was another tree on my right, peculiarly appearing to be growing atop a 3 ft thick slab of limestone. It was beneath this rock that the creature had vanished. Pushing my long walking stick into the hole as far as I could, I noticed that behind the seemingly small frontal space there seemed to be a cavern. This is not surprising given the nature of the Mendip Hills.

One is left to wonder what I saw, but if you talk to the locals at the White Hart public house in Cross they might be willing to tell you about the mythical beast of Cross – but to them it is no myth. Some seem to think that the creature might be an escaped large carnivorous cat of some kind and they will swear to you that they have seen it, and not only at closing time.

16

Carry on walking through the wood and eventually you will emerge out of it. The track then narrows considerably, but you carry on. Eventually you come to a small wooden gate leading into a little lane. Walk on down the lane to reach the village of Cross.

4. Turn right on the metalled road, walking past the village pub. After about a further ½ mile you will come to a T-junction and on your left is Old Coach Road, heading towards the village of Weare. Turn left here, following the road on down to the stream and the aptly named 'Bow Bridge'.

5. Turn right over the stile into the field beyond, keeping the shallow river on your right and following it downstream. The river is full of small fish and because it is so straight and shallow you may occasionally glimpse a swirl of water as a pike makes an attack on one of them – and if you are lucky you might actually spot the pike. Carry on along the footpath, ignoring the first footbridge on your right. Eventually you will come out into a small lane. Turn right and cross over the bridge, following the track up to a metalled road.

6. Turn left on this road and continue through what remains of the village of Rackley. Looking at it now, it is hard to imagine that this was once a thriving Roman and medieval port, from which the principal cargos of lead, made up into heavy iron ingots called pigs, and calamine were exported. Similarly, manufactured goods and coal from Wales arrived here by sea. All this ended in 1802 when the floodgates at Bleadon were installed (see Walk 1); although there were some lock gates, they were too small for the larger barges to pass through.

Keep walking along this road until it peters out, then go through the metal gate ahead and into a field. Keeping the hedge on your left, follow the footpath along. You then cross a track running from right to left and down to the Old River Axe. Go over a stile into the field ahead of you. Again, keep the hedge on your left, and walk on as far as you can go. You leave the final field by a stile in the top left-hand corner. Turn right on the track and follow it along. Eventually it opens up into a metalled road lined with large houses, some with unusual architectural features. This lane is called Kennel Lane, which is not surprising as you will be passing large dog kennels on your left. At the end of the lane, go right to return to the hotel.

CHEDDAR
The Riverside Inn
❧❀❧

This route begins at the bottom end of the Cheddar Gorge itself, moving upwards by means of a footpath and following the rim of this world famous gorge. The views obtained are simply spectacular and show off the natural beauty of the Mendip countryside to its best advantage. Topping the rise the walk then descends through a small forest littered with wild fungi before entering the Black Rock Nature Reserve. The trail goes back along the other side of the gorge and then follows the road down into the tourist heart of Cheddar, revealing a view of the steep sides that cannot normally be appreciated when travelling by car.

The Riverside Inn in Cheddar is located at the foot of the gorge and alongside the pretty river that rises from the caves about 500 yards up the road and from which it takes its name. To the rear of the inn there is a large and attractive garden. Despite its proximity to the tourist part of the gorge the Riverside still retains the feel of a local village pub and extends a friendly welcome to walkers. On the day that I visited three real ales and draught Guinness were on offer as well as the normal range of lagers and cask beers.

There is an extremely varied menu along with blackboard specials. Main meals include neck of lamb fillet and Somerset chicken, and by far the most requested meal is apparently the steak and Guinness pie. Responsible dog owners are very welcome in the bar and in the riverside garden. The inn also has a separate non-smoking restaurant area.

To find out the bar opening hours or to book a meal you should telephone 01934 742452. Alternatively, you could visit http://www.riversidecheddar.co.uk where you can also get details of special wine and food offers.

- **HOW TO GET THERE:** Cheddar is reached on the A371 north-west of Wells. Turn onto the B3135 and follow the road signs for Cheddar Gorge. At the T-junction the inn is on your right.
- **PARKING:** There is parking available at the inn, for which a small charge is made, refundable to patrons. A very large public car park is adjacent.
- **LENGTH OF THE WALK:** 3 miles. Map: OS Explorer 141 Cheddar Gorge and Mendip Hills West (GR 461536).

THE WALK

1. Leave the inn and turn right, walking over the river bridge. Turn immediately right and start walking up the lane, keeping St Andrew's Road to your right. After about 300 yards turn left into Lynch Lane. In 100 yards or so you need to keep your eyes open for the footpath. The lane you are walking up branches right along a bridleway opposite a car parking space. In front of you will be the double metal gates of Glen View. Just behind the car parking space on your left the footpath goes up through the wood. Follow the well-marked track up through the wood until you come to another track. On the left is a large look-out tower with 47 steps, from which you get a fantastic view across the Cheddar Valley and over to the Bristol Channel.

2. With your back to the tower, walk on ahead, ignoring the concreted path and steps that soon fall away to your left and back down into the gorge. The footpath goes uphill, keeping the gorge close on your left-hand side. There are frequent places to stop and gaze down into it as you

19

move upwards, or you can turn around to admire the spectacular view unfolding behind you. The walker passes through areas of woodland with an abundance of young ash trees and shrubs, the path going through high gorse and ferns. When I did this walk in summer the ferns were alive with butterflies, particularly the small tortoiseshells.

A favourite place to stop is at the top of the gorge, with a steep drop away to your left and the best view obtainable anywhere in the Mendips presenting itself behind you.

Follow the path downhill and soon you join the West Mendip Way, with signposts pointing towards Shipham. Follow this track down and enter an older wood with more mature ash and oak trees.

3. As you get towards the bottom of the slope you will hear cars passing down the Cheddar Gorge in front of you. The footpath goes straight on ahead steeply downhill (ignore this) but also bears sharply round to your right. Follow this right-hand path and soon you will arrive at the B3135, opposite the Black Rock Nature Reserve. Cross over the road and enter the reserve through the kissing gate. Start walking up the miniature gorge. Old trees such as oaks and yews are much in evidence here, although most of the former now appear to be rotting tree trunks on the ground. The rocks are thickly covered in green moss, almost hiding the limestone from view.

4. After about 100 yards you come to a wooden gate. Go through the gate and bear sharp left back up the hill, following the signpost towards Cheddar. Walking up a gentle incline takes you through a patch of hazelnut trees before you come surprisingly upon a small and ancient meadow on your right-hand side. The meadow brown butterflies appear to dominate this area in season. Another surprise, in the form of a magnificent Mendips stone stile, with the stones set into the wall in the shape of steps, greets the walker. Ahead will be a steep incline with steps cut into it; ignore this. Go over the stile and turn immediately left. Having turned left, follow the track downhill, leaving it by means of a stile before arriving at the road ahead.

5. Turn right and walk back down through the picturesque Cheddar Gorge itself. This gives one a chance to get a truer perspective on its height and magnificence. It is surprising how narrow the gorge really is. Follow the road down and you will pass the entrance to what was a cave behind a small car park. The television programme Time Team

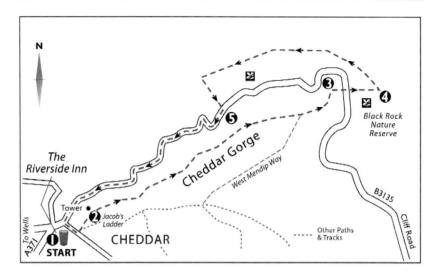

excavated this cave and found evidence of Stone Age occupation. Long ago the cave extended out into where the road now is, before the ravages of time eroded its entrance away. Back in 1968 a savage flood washed tons of debris into the cave and choked it up, leaving mostly what you see now.

Carry on down the road and you will arrive at the commercial heart of the gorge, complete with the world famous caves. These are open to the public to visit, for a price. For further information check out the caves' website at http://www.cheddarcaves.co.uk. Pass the famous Cheddar cheese shop on your right-hand side and walk back over the river bridge to where you parked your car.

SHIPHAM

The Penscot Inn
⊷⊱⊱⊶

This walk starts at the very pretty former mining village of Shipham. Passing through Rowberrow Warren, a large wood, the walker moves ever gently uphill before arriving at the Burrington Commons. Here a reminder of the Second World War comes starkly into focus in the shape of an unexpected air raid shelter. The route moves up to the highest point of the Mendips, Beacon Batch, without the walker actually noticing the ascent. It is here that a marvellous reward awaits you. Breathtakingly beautiful views across the whole of the Mendips and over the Bristol Channel are there for the taking, and remain so as the route leaves Beacon Batch and returns to Shipham via the small village of Rowberrow.

The Penscot Inn is the newest secret of the Mendips and is an excellent place for refreshement before or after the walk. Originally built round about the year 1450, it was traditionally a coaching inn. Until recently it was known as the Farmers Hotel and Restaurant and it did not present itself as a local pub to drink or socialise in. These days, however, it is an inn and restaurant with a superb public bar and two separate eating areas. The extensive menu caters for all styles of eating. Meals include chicken tikka masala with rice, steak and ale pie and several sizzler dishes, such as steak. In addition freshly made sandwiches are always available. Vegetarian food is served too. Three real ales are offered, along with Guinness, local cider and the standard range of cask ales and lagers. Outside, the pretty garden is very safe and secure for young children. The pub is dog friendly and extends a special welcome to walkers. Telephone: 01934 842659.

- **HOW TO GET THERE:** From the A38 between Bridgwater and Bristol, turn eastwards on the road signed 'Shipham ½', about 17 miles from Bridgwater. At the next T-junction, turn right into the village of Shipham. The Penscot Inn is immediately beyond the village butcher's shop, set back in a dip to the right.
- **PARKING:** There is plenty of parking available at the inn.
- **LENGTH OF THE WALK:** 7½ miles. Map: OS Explorer 141 Cheddar Gorge and Mendip Hills West (GR 444575).

THE WALK

1. Walk out of the inn and cross over the road in front of you and onto Hollow Road, keeping the war memorial and the pretty village green on your left. Follow the minor road up through the village. On the day I passed by a lady came out of one of the cottages on my right and vigorously pumped water out of an old-fashioned water pump. Obviously it was still in regular use. Where the road takes a definite left-hand bend, walk straight ahead and up the lane called Barn Pool. At the next T-junction, turn right and walk along the metalled Lippiatt Lane. After a time this lane becomes a Y-shaped fork, with the last house for a while on your left. Take the left-hand metalled road and follow it up. There is a bridleway sign bearing the legend 'Shipham and the West Mendip Way' that points the direction you need to take. At the very top of the track you come to another T-junction with a house on the right. Cross over, going slightly to the right, and enter Rowberrow Warren along a sunken track with trees on either side. This is a well-marked track and goes downhill to a small stream at the bottom. Cross over the stream.

2. Turn right after crossing the stream, keeping the covered Bristol Waterworks reservoir on your right. Follow the well-marked track,

23

ignoring another track joining from the left. A lovely view opens up to the other side of the valley. Foxgloves and ferns embellish both sides of the track, with common brown and tortoiseshell butterflies, and the odd small white butterfly, flitting between the flowers searching for a meal in summer. At the next track crossroads, head straight across and follow the signs for Cheddar. An old limestone wall will appear on your right as you leave Rowberrow Warren behind you. Follow the track along and go out onto a minor country lane after passing through the Tyning Trekking Centre.

3. At the road, turn left and walk along it for about ½ mile. You will pass an entrance to Pineysleight and Charterhouse farms on your right. The road then goes downhill for about 100 yards before you meet a small layby on your right. On your left you will find a pedestrian wooden gate. Go through this and walk up the very short lane. At its end, cross over to the field in front of you. Angle slightly to your right across this field. Follow the small track and head towards the radio masts that will appear as you go uphill. Go through the metal gate and into the next field, but this time angling left towards a visible mound.

This is no ordinary mound, but a remnant of a command post used during the Mendips' secret war and connected with an operation called 'Starfish'. It is an old air raid shelter, still open to the weather and casual visitor. During the war the area in front of you was used as a decoy site for enemy bombers, to divert fire from Bristol, and the RAF personnel involved often had to take shelter at this spot.

Go through the wooden pedestrian gate in front of you and onto Burrington Common. Turn right and walk along the track, heading towards the large radio masts and keeping the fields on your right. Look out for the beautiful pink heathers and a purple plant, somewhat like a heather, but locally named 'ling'. You also pass through a small but unexpected boggy area containing sedge grasses.

4. At the next track crossroads, go left and walk gently uphill. The two radio masts will now be directly behind you.

5. Surprisingly this gentle walk uphill delivers you to the highest point of the Mendips, Beacon Batch. This is marked by a white concrete trig point, used by the Ordnance Survey mapmakers and recorded as being 325 metres or 1,068 feet above sea level. Your splendid reward for taking this walk is the spectacular and beautiful views that unfold before

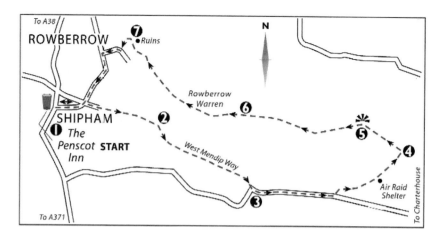

you. On a fine day most of the Bristol Channel spreads before the walker. Other noteworthy views are Wales, distantly ahead, Exmoor off to your left and Bristol away to the right. On most clear days you can also see both of the Severn bridges, while on an exceptionally clear day you can see the Malvern Hills far away to your right. The large expanse of the Chew Magna reservoir is also in sight on your right. Local people have named this spot 'two blankets', because whatever the weather elsewhere on the Mendips you will need another two blankets at Beacon Batch.

Look around and you will notice small rounded humps – ancient burial barrows. Even the trig point on which you are standing is placed on a barrow. Just behind you, the nearest barrow to you was the site of a gibbet. Poor unfortunates were usually hung in chains at this spot, local legend placing the last execution here at about 1818. The main road from Charterhouse to Bristol once passed in front of this point and the gibbet was a sombre reminder to travellers, particularly the noted hard and rough lead miners of the day, of the ultimate price to be paid for breaking the law.

In front of you there are two well-marked paths. Take the left-hand path (locally known as the Slaggers' Path), where tradition has it that miners used to walk from Shipham to Charterhouse and thence to their place of work. During the Second World War lorries used to labour up this path to place heaps of stone and rubble (known as tumps) on the plateau to prevent airborn assaults by enemy troops. Continue along the ridge of Burrington Common and head towards the wood in the distance. Where the well-used track forks, take the right-hand track and

The view from Beacon Batch, the highest point on the Mendips

walk towards the island of Flat Holm far off in the Bristol Channel. At the first track crossroads, go straight across and head for the wood.

6. Go through the pedestrian wooden gate and into wooded Rowberrow Warren again. At the first track crossroads, walk straight ahead until you come to a T-junction. Make sure that you take the right-hand track and walk downhill. The next junction is a little tricky. Ignore the first and second tracks on the left but take the large and obvious one straight ahead on the right. Ignore any other tracks and stay on this wide hardcore track that opens out to the size of a small road, following it downhill for quite a way.

7. Just before the ruined cottage and outbuildings that appear on your right, turn left. Follow the signpost that marks the way to Rowberrow. At the next T-junction go left again, still following the signpost to Rowberrow. This brings you out into a small lane, where you turn right. Continue up to the next T-junction, with the unexpected Swan Inn on your right. Turn left here and follow the minor road back down through Rowberrow Lane and into Shipham, via Hollow Road. The inn is just across the road from you at the T-junction.

BURRINGTON COMBE
The Burrington Inn
❧❀❧

This circular walk goes through beautiful Mendip Lodge Wood and passes the remains of the lodge itself. It then moves up to the National Trust property of Dolebury Warren and its large Iron Age fort before visiting a hidden pothole, Rod's Pot, and continuing in an easterly direction along the rim of the famous Burrington Combe. The route returns down the picturesque combe itself and passes impressive Aveline's Hole, one of the deeper Mendip caves. Nearby is the rock formation where a local pastor penned the hymn 'Rock of Ages' as he took shelter from a thunderstorm.

The Burrington Inn strangely does not lie in the village of Burrington, but about ½ mile to the south-west of it, in Burrington Combe. Originally the building was not a pub at all, but a café catering for the visitors to the combe. In the late 1940s/early 1950s, it obtained a liquor licence and from there developed into the inn and restaurant it is today. Even odder is the fact that the pub is not shown on the OS map for the area.

The inn is well known locally and is popular with walkers and cavers. Besides the standard range of beers and lagers, there is at always at least one real ale on offer. On the day that I visited this was the locally produced Butcombe Bitter. The inn has an excellent reputation for its solid array of good and substantial meals, from steaks through to salads, and there is an extensive range of sandwiches. A small separate dining area is available, also tables and chairs outside for those who wish to eat in the fresh air. Dogs (except guide dogs) are not allowed into the pub but are welcome outside. Telephone: 01761 462227.

- **How to get there:** From the A38 between Bridgwater and Bristol, turn eastwards onto the A368 just south of the village of Lower Langford. After about 2 miles, turn right onto the B3134. The Burrington Inn is located on the left, just after the garden centre and just as you begin to enter the combe itself.
- **Parking:** There is ample parking at the inn.
- **Length of the walk:** 7 miles. Map: OS Explorer 141 Cheddar Gorge and Mendip Hills West (GR 477591).

The Walk

1. Leave the inn and turn right. Walk downhill along the road, keeping the garden centre immediately to your right. At the road sign 'Ham Link' cross over to the lane with the dead end signpost. A gentle walk uphill through a shady lane suddenly opens up to offer a splendid and sweeping view across the valley on your right. As you admire this view, look out for the footpath immediately on your right where the wood starts. Follow this well-marked footpath into the private mixed woodland planted in the 19th century, Mendip Lodge Wood. Everywhere laurel shrubs wrestle with the rough outcrops of limestone in an attempt to dominate the landscape. The occasional smell of rotting meat draws your attention to the unusual stinkhorn fungus. Its scent attracts flies which, after landing upon the sticky source of the smell, carry away the spores of the fungus to propagate elsewhere.

2. After a while you will come across the impressive remains of a large stately house built at the end of the 18th century – Mendip Lodge – after which the wood was named. Lovely arched stone window frames and fire hearths remain intact. Mysterious doorways lead down invitingly into the darkness of the cellars, but do not be tempted. If you have children, please do not let them attempt to explore the ruins as

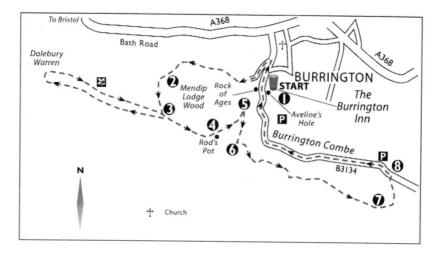

they are in a dangerous state. Walking along the track, take the first left turn and start to move uphill. After about 100 yards, the track you are following carries on straight ahead, but the footpath bears right by an old yew tree and leads quickly into a sunken lane with walls on both sides. Turn left.

3. Where the lane leaves the wood, you will find another footpath joining from the right. Take this footpath onto Dolebury Warren. Follow the well-marked path along through the pine and blackthorn plantation and walk right to the end and into the approximately 20 acre site of an Iron Age fort. On a clear day the highest point of the fort offers spectacular views across to the Bristol Channel, with the islands of Flat Holm and Steep Holm in view.

Return the way you came to the point where you left the footpath. Turn right here and walk on up the track, keeping the barbed wire fence on the left at all times, until you come to a noticeable depression in the landscape on your right-hand side.

4. Look carefully and you will see a track hidden by large ferns that will lead you down to the bottom of this deep depression. Follow the track down and suddenly before you the entrance to a hidden pothole typical of the Mendips appears – Rod's Pot. Please note the warning sign that indicates that even experienced cavers can get into trouble. Go back up to the path and follow it down to your right. In approximately 50 yards you will see yet another depression on your right. Return to the track and continue down it, ignoring the track coming from the private house on your left.

5. At the next track junction, opposite the wooden house and farm gate, turn right, going gently uphill.

6. At the track crossroads, turn left, keeping the hill on your right. Ahead and away to your left you will see the clear limestone escarpment of Burrington Combe. Follow this track. You will pass over a stream, and if it is wet the stream will be flowing across the track. If dry, you can walk up it for about 50 yards and see the water disappear underground. Continue along the path ignoring two paths joining from the right.

7. About 20 feet beyond where the second path joins from the right, move off the main path and go left. Walk downhill between fields on your left and right and down to the metalled road. You are now at the top of Burrington Combe.

8. Turn left here and walk down the road, facing the traffic. Continue through the combe. After a while, cross over the road and onto a track that leads downhill and on through a small wooded area. Where the track comes out of the trees, on your right, you will find the magnificent Aveline's Hole. The remains of prehistoric man have been found here and the cave is an important one in the Mendips. It angles down steeply, and if you do not have the right boots on you can easily slip on the deceptively wet surface, so take care. Having had a good look, walk back across the road.

After about 100 yards, you will come across a steep crevice in the rock on your left. A metal plaque recounts how the Reverend A.M. Toplady, whilst taking shelter from a savage storm sometime between 1762–65, was inspired to write the hymn 'Rock of Ages' on a playing card as he waited. Walk back down the road and cross over to the Burrington Inn.

BLAGDON
The New Inn
❦

The very pretty village of Blagdon is unusual in that it is split into three distinct parts: Street End, West End and East End. This is a lovely walk along country lanes, down into Nether Wood and the beautiful Blackmoor Reserve. It then moves on to Charterhouse, with its nearby Roman fort and settlement, through Velvet Bottom and back to Blagdon, with spectacular views across the valley to the lake.

In Victorian times Blagdon was a mining town with six pubs, of which four now remain. The 17th century New Inn has a car park with a magnificent view that most people would give their eye teeth for – set up on the hill, the view is unrivalled. This is also a pub that is well known locally for the quality of its food, with plenty of home-made specials available – on the day I visited these were game pie and steak and kidney pie. There is also a 'Kids Korner' menu.

Three real ales are usually on offer, together with draught Guinness and a range of other beers and lagers. Dogs are welcome but only in the garden. Telephone: 01761 462475.

• **How to get there:** Take the A368, which runs between the A38 at Churchill and the A37 west of Bath. Turn off by the school in Blagdon, opposite the Live and Let Live pub. Follow the road down and the New Inn is on the right opposite the church.

• **Parking:** There is ample parking at the inn.

• **Length of the walk:** 8 miles. Map: OS Explorer 141 Cheddar Gorge and Mendip Hills West (GR 505589).

The Walk

1. Leave the pub and walk up Park Lane and into Church Street, walking up the road and leaving the church behind you to your right. At the main road, cross over, and keep the Live and Let Live on your right. Walk up Score Lane. Continue straight ahead and go off the metalled road onto a track, keeping the stone hut on your right. Go over the stile and up the lane. After about 50 yards, cross another stile, and after another 20 yards the footpath splits left and right. Take the left-hand path, very soon coming out into an open field. Go across this field diagonally left towards a stunted beech tree in the top left-hand corner. You are now on the Mendips plateau. Cross over the stile into the field and walk straight ahead, keeping the hedge on your left. Quite soon you will come to a metalled farm track with the farm on your left.

2. Walk straight over the track and into Leaze Lane. When you come to a stile across the lane, cross it into the field, keeping the hedge immediately on your left until you arrive at a metalled track.

3. Cross over the stile into Ubley Drove and turn right. On reaching the road, go straight across it and over the stile into the field. Keep the hedge on the right all the way towards the wood ahead.

4. Go over the stile into Nether Wood, following the small track through until you meet a proper man-made track. Follow this track round to your right, into the Blackmoor Nature Reserve. Keeping to the right-hand track at all times, you come across a preserved remnant of the mining days, the condenser flues from a lead processing factory. Keep on the track until you come to a car park. Turn right, heading towards the tip of a church tower that you can see ahead. Walk up this track, by now metalled, to the crossroads, with the Charterhouse Centre on your left. Before you move on from here, it is worth detouring to your right for about 50 yards to gateways with explanatory posters.

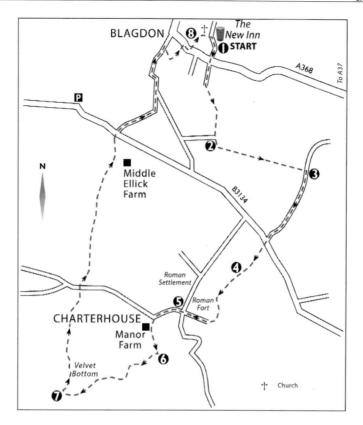

5. Go back to the crossroads. There is a road signpost pointing towards Shipham. Go right along this road and down into what remains of Charterhouse. As you come into the village (a few houses and farms), you will see a pond on your left within some wooded ground. There are in fact two ponds, and between them is an old Mendips arched bridge. Going over this bridge, walk through the wooded ground and out into the field beyond.

Keeping Manor Farm on the right, walk along the field with the very high Mendip stone wall on your right. Go over the stile at the little wood, walking up towards the track and a building - the Mendip Adventure Base.

6. Turn right here and walk along the nature reserve trail through Velvet Bottom. Lead mining was much in evidence here during Roman times, and later the Victorians reprocessed what was left. The flat bottom of the valley is pitted with holes and excavations, but after a while you drop down on terraces. These are the remains of a series of dams, buddles (tanks in which lead ore was washed and graded) and settling beds that fills the lower end of Velvet Bottom.

7. Walk down this lovely valley until you reach its end. Do not leave through the wooden gates, but go right up the side of the hill and head towards the right side of the wood that appears before you. Go over the stile and, keeping the wood on your left, follow it for one field. Cross the stile into the next field, angling right towards the wall. Go down into the corner, crossing the stile into the next field. Angle right, to the top right-hand corner, heading towards a house in the distance on your right. Drop down along the track, keeping the house on the right. Cross a small stream by the footbridge before coming out onto a metalled road.

Turn right and then almost immediately left over the stile and into the field. Keeping the deep stream gully on your left, walk until you come to a stile. Go over the stile and walk up the field, keeping the wire fence on your right. Where the fence goes right, walk straight ahead. As you continue up the hill you will see the scar of the stream on your left. Make your way to where the stream meets a stile and track on your left, and cross over into the field beyond.

Go straight ahead over the field, keeping the wire fence on your left. Walk down the hill, with the rough ground and deep ravine on your left. Continue until you come out onto a farm track, with the farm immediately on your right. Go over the stile and walk straight ahead, keeping the farm on your right, and head towards the wood. Follow the metalled track to the B3134. Go straight over the crossroads, signposted to Blagdon. Follow this minor road down to the next T-junction and turn left into the village. Very shortly you come to a viewpoint on your right.

Walk on down the road. At the first T-junction, turn right into Street End Lane. After 200 yards, with Stoney Batch cottage on your left, turn left down a narrow grassy lane and follow this to the main road.

8. Turn right. Just past Eldreds Orchard on the left, is a footpath. Go through the kissing gate and take the higher of the two paths. Keep the house on your right and continue to the church, where you turn right and walk out to Park Lane and The New Inn.

DRAYCOTT
The Strawberry Special
✦❀✦

This very easy route begins on the southern slopes of the Mendips at Draycott, arguably the strawberry growing capital of England. Having left the unusually named pub, and following the long-abandoned Cheddar railway line, the walker passes over an extremely rare 'double' bridge. The circuit is mostly along flat ground until it reaches what was once the outlying mystical island of Nyland, with its connections to the legendary King Arthur. Around the bottom of Nyland Hill the walker experiences a landscape of gruffs (i.e. trenches which follow the lines of lead excavations), before returning by way of what was once a large decoy pool for wildfowl and back to the Strawberry Special, taking in a surprise visit to the former village station right at the end of the walk.

The infamous rail cuts made in the 1960s because of Dr Beeching's recommendations led to the Railway Inn being renamed the Strawberry Special in 1963 to commemorate the local name given to a steam train

35

that used to haul the strawberry crop up to Covent Garden during the growing season. What was once the station is literally a stone's throw away across the village road and easily recognisable because its front gate looks remarkably like an old level crossing gate.

Outside the pub, there is a small walled garden shaded by an enormous old walnut tree that has its own resident population of woodpeckers – they are almost certain to be there when you visit. One can also see a set of steps that appear to go nowhere. These were used by customers to mount their horses after a visit to the pub in pre-motoring days.

Talk to the landlord about the ghosts that frequent the area – there are two. One is a ghost in the bar, reputed to be harmless, but insisting on walking around after closing time. The other claim is that on some clear nights the sound of the Strawberry Special can be heard pulling out from the old station.

This is a real village pub that extends a friendly welcome to walkers. On the day that I visited three real ales and Guinness were on offer. The bar food ranges from ham, egg and chips to toasties. Local pasties obtained from the village butcher are also available. Responsible dog owners are welcome in the bar and the garden. Telephone: 01934 742177.

> • **HOW TO GET THERE:** Draycott is on the A371 between Cheddar and Wells. Turn off opposite the war memorial and follow the road down to the T-junction. The Strawberry Special is on your left.
> • **PARKING:** There is parking available at the pub and on the road outside.
> • **LENGTH OF THE WALK:** 3½ miles. Map: OS Explorer 141 Cheddar Gorge and Mendip Hills West (GR 475506).

THE WALK

1. Leave the pub and cross the road to the station house. Turn right, ignoring the road you came down, and walk straight ahead. Within 100 yards you come to a turning on your left. Ignore this and walk on along the village lane, following the road round to your right and into Back Lane. In front of you will be the main Mendip Hills. After about 300 yards turn left into Westfield Lane.

2. At the road junction, turn left. After about another 100 yards, at the bend, note the very interesting gatepost. Limestone gateposts were once in common use in this part of the world. It is perhaps not

36

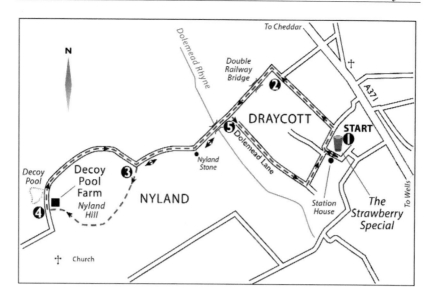

surprising that some people might mistake them for standing stones, particularly if one or two are left standing alone together or singly in the middle of a field.

Follow the road round and pass over the old Great Western Railway line by means of the very interesting bridge. One side was for road traffic whilst the other was for the movement of farm animals. Note the use of old steel railway rails cut into the form of durable fenceposts on the end of the bridge. Walk on up the road and over the rhyne (a small man-made waterfall) and the magical island of Nyland Hill rises up invitingly out of the Levels, but before reaching them a portion of limestone suddenly seems to jump out of the earth at you, forming a razor-like narrow ridge called Nyland Stone. It is easy to visualise the water lapping around this back in the time of Alfred the Great. Follow the road around to your right. Beautiful old Batts Farm appears on your left, together with some fine outbuildings. The whole farm is complemented by a very pretty garden. Walk on along the road to where it bends to the right.

3. Go left here along the track, keeping the red postbox set in the wall on your left. Follow the track on round and through some gates, passing Rookery Farm. Walk up the small lane and out into the field beyond. Keeping the hedge on your left, walk around the bottom of Nyland Hill, which looms mysteriously up above you. Local legend has it that this hill is a man-made fort, specifically built for defensive purposes. It was used as a beacon point in the old days, and if you look across to the left you can see Glastonbury Tor in the distance. These places both stand on the mysterious ley line that connects St Michael's Mount in Cornwall to Stonehenge on Salisbury Plain (see also Walk 16). It is not hard to imagine King Alfred visiting this part of his defences or to visualise the Viking and Danish raiders of yore heading up towards Glastonbury in their long ships, intent on pillage and destruction.

The bottom of the hill is pockmarked with the remains of gruffs that have returned to nature – gruffy ground – and other small quarry-like depressions. Some limestone rocks are beginning to assert themselves through the red earth, whilst digging by badgers exposes what could be an internal cave system. Small pockets of white marble-like rock cling to the side of some of the limestone outcrops. Follow the footpath on around the bottom of the hill and keep the hedge on your left, eventually leaving by way of a stile back onto the small country lane.

4. Turn right. On your right you pass the aptly named Decoy Pool Farm. To the left of the road and opposite the farm, you can just make out the remains of a large pool. At the far end of the hedge along the road, willows and rushes still mark its furthest extent. In this decoy pool a great number of wild ducks, mallards, teal, wigeon and pintails to name but a few, were lured to their fate by experienced wildfowlers down throughout the ages. Continue round to point 3 and follow the road back the way you came.

5. About 200 yards after you have passed the rhyne, turn right over the stile onto the track. Just before its end there is a private drive that leads you behind the station house. The current owners have a right of way along here and they are happy for you to walk along it to take a photograph. The building was once the ticket office and waiting room of Draycott Station, from where the Strawberry Special train used to depart.

At the top of the lane turn right to return to the pub.

PRIDDY
The Queen Victoria Inn
❧❦❧

The Queen Victoria is within a minute of the world famous and picturesque Priddy village green. This is the highest village in the Mendips and one of the very few left on the plateau. Passing the green and its unique thatched stack of hurdles, the walk heads off in a south-westerly direction along the very top of the hills. From there, the walk reaches a scene of absolute beauty, with far reaching views of the Wiltshire border, Exmoor, Wales and the Bristol Channel. This pleasant route on ground that is generally fairly level then follows the line of some cattle droves back towards the village.

The Queen Victoria did not become an inn until 1851. Prior to that it is believed to have been two separate buildings. Inside there are three open fires that are usually lit in cold weather. Internally, the bar area has an old look and feel about it, with strong wooden bench seats and tables much in evidence. Outside, there is a large garden across the road, with a substantial children's play area. A small walled patio area is just outside the pub.

The inn is well used to walkers and has an extensive range of sandwiches and ploughman's available, also substantial pub fare such as cod in crisp batter, sausage and chips, pizzas and quiches. Children's meals are also served. When I visited there were three real ales on offer, as well as traditional farmhouse cider, Guinness and the usual range of cask bitters and lagers. The pub is very dog friendly. Telephone: 01749 676385.

- **How to get there:** Priddy is signposted from the A39, about 3½ miles north of Wells. In the village, turn left into Pelting Drove to find the Queen Victoria.
- **Parking:** There is ample parking at the inn.
- **Length of the walk:** The short route is 3 miles and the full route is 6 miles. Map: OS Explorer 141 Cheddar Gorge and Mendip Hills West (GR 528508).

The Walk

1. Leave the inn and go straight ahead to the T-junction. Turn left. Walk a short way up to the village green triangle, turning left by the New Inn. Keeping the inn on your left, walk up to the end of the green, the site of the famous and ancient Priddy Fair. The building on the green is actually a store for old hurdles that were once used to contain animals for sale.

At the end of the village green triangle, at the crossroads, turn left and walk up the metalled track past the no-through road signs. Where the lane finishes, go over the wooden stile and into the field beyond. Walk across the fields straight ahead. Shortly you will come to a triangular shaped wood on your left, and a large depression in the ground that is a pond. This is surprising because on the porous ground of the Mendips plateau water was usually hard to store. If you look carefully at the near side of the pond, you should be able to see stone walls set on each side of a small depression leading into it. A large slab of limestone seals off the end, giving the whole affair a small 'n' shape. In this 'n' the cattle could safely drink and not wander any further out into the deep pond. Modernisation has not seen the need to keep this pond in action any more and the water has mostly leaked away. A metal water trough now suffices.

Carry on straight across the field, following the obvious tracks over the stiles. As you walk along the plateau, an exceptionally fine view opens up. Away to your left you can see as far away as the Wiltshire border, whilst Exmoor looms ahead of you. The nuclear power plant at

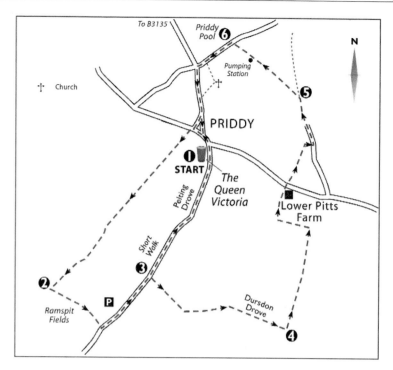

Hinkley Point stands out as a solid slab next to the sea. Away to your right lies the Bristol Channel and Wales.

2. As you start to descend from the plateau, you come to a wooden stile with a stone stile on the left. The ground to your left has no public footpath but these 48 acres are owned by Somerset County Council and form part of the Countryside Stewardship Scheme. You are free to roam through this area.

Go over the stone stile. Ahead you will notice a car park on the ridge in the distance. Below you and slightly to the right is a building. Behind this is an area of very rough ground known as Ramspit Fields, the remains of a long abandoned medieval farm. Head towards the car park and follow the faint track, which then dips down and becomes an obvious track. Follow this out to the road and turn left. Walk up to the car park, with its information board. As you go, look out for buzzards and kestrels making use of the air currents blowing strongly up the hill.

Leave the car park behind you and walk on up the incline. Very shortly you will pass a farm building on your right, and about 50 yards later, on your left, there is another fine example of a water pit, which would have been lined with flat limestone and clay. Continue along this road and pass Moor View on your left, very soon coming to a track on your right leading down to Ebbor Grove Farm.

If you are taking the short version of the walk, all you have to do is continue along this road for less than a mile and you will come to the Queen Victoria.

3. For the longer walk, turn right and head towards Ebbor Grove Farm. Pass the farm and 200 yards later the track bears sharply around to the left and narrows. At the next track junction, ignore the footpath to the left and continue straight ahead on the wider track. This is known as Dursdon Drove.

4. At the next track junction go left over the cattle grid and through the metal gates along a very well made up track, following it all the way along until it reaches the minor road by the farm. Go straight over the road and through the stone stile into the field beyond. There is a wooden signpost indicating East Water Lane and Priddy church. Walk straight ahead, keeping the limestone wall on your left. Just before you go through the caravan park, it is worthwhile noting the footpath to your left. About 100 yards further up you will see the rough ground where North Hill Swallet lies. A swallet is a place where water from a surface stream sinks underground.

Go right and pass through the caravan park. Continue to the metalled track. Turn left and walk up the lane. Very shortly the metalled track gives way to a grassy drove.

5. After about 75 yards, go left over a stile into a field. Angle right, heading to the right of the pump house in a small wood in the distance. Go over the stone stile into the wooded area and follow the track up to the road and turn left.

6. Walk along the road, passing the famous Priddy Pool on your right. Turn left at the junction; a signpost points the way to Wells. Walk across the village green, passing the hurdle stack, and back to your car.

WALK 9

WOOKEY HOLE
The Wookey Hole Inn
◆◆◆

*T̶his short walk takes in the heart of the Mendips and the amazing
source of the River Axe. Starting at the famous Wookey Hole Inn the
route leads into the stunningly beautiful and tranquil National Trust
area of Ebbor Gorge on a well-trodden path, with a magnificent view
from a gloriously steep precipice at the top. From there the trail circles
back down to the beginning of the gorge before returning to the inn.*

Wookey Hole village itself nestles in the peaceful bosom of the
Mendips. Its two most notable attractions are the Wookey Hole Caves
and the Paper Mill. Both are today a tourist attraction in their own right
but, of the two, the caves are perhaps the more famous. Legend has it
that an old crone, a witch, lived in the Wookey Hole until a monk from
nearby Glastonbury Abbey turned her into stone. This seems to have
been supported when excavations in the early part of the 20th century
discovered the skeleton of a woman deep in the floor. What was so
interesting about this skeleton was that she was supposedly found

43

with a sacrificial knife and a round stalagmite that looked not unlike a crystal ball.

The popular Wookey Hole Inn has a Mediterranean theme, and also claims to have the largest selection of Belgian beers in the country. In addition there are at least four real ales on the pumps at any one time, with the local Wook Ale always available. The inn also has an excellent reputation for food. When I visited, the dishes ranged from pasta with grilled vegetables and olives to roasted rack of marinated lamb. Snacks such as sandwiches and chips are always available. Outside there is a large walled garden with tables. Walkers are welcome as are responsible dog owners.

The inn's website is www.wookeyholeinn.com. It is always advisable to book a table if you want a meal here. Telephone: 01749 676677.

- **HOW TO GET THERE:** Take the A371 between Cheddar and Wells. The road is well signposted to Wookey Hole from whichever direction you travel. The inn is located in the centre of the village.
- **PARKING:** There is ample parking opposite the inn.
- **LENGTH OF THE WALK:** 3 miles. Map: OS Explorer 141 Cheddar Gorge and Mendip Hills West (GR 532476).

THE WALK

1. Leave the Wookey Hole Inn and turn right. Walk along the road, keeping the large car park for the caves on your left. Also on your left there is a fast flowing stream that emerges from underneath the road via a tunnel by the cave entrance. It then passes under the remains of an original bridge, a single arch that now connects to a building. If you walk quietly and slowly up to the stream and peer into its deeper parts you will see the silver flash of small trout as they dart for cover. Although it does not look much at this point, this is actually the start of the River Axe, whose source is within the Wookey Hole cave system. The river continues on to eventually flow into the Bristol Channel at Uphill, just to the south of Weston-Super-Mare.

As you walk past the road leading to the entrance to the caves, note the old road sign on your left that states 'This road is not suitable for charabancs'. Walk through the village until you come to its outskirts. At the white metal Wookey Hole village sign, turn right through a metal kissing gate and follow the track along for a short way.

2. At the bottom of the hill, turn left and follow the track. There is a

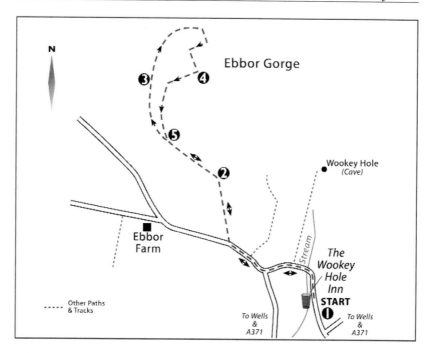

wooden signpost indicating 'Priddy 3 miles'. Keep the hedge on your left. Enter the wood over the wooden stile. Look carefully at the larger tree trunks and you will notice some bird nesting boxes occasionally affixed to them. Follow the path until it splits into three ways. Take the centre path that bears the legend 'The Gorge'. Follow the well-made track on up and pass through the beautiful Ebbor Gorge. This was carved out of the limestone by a prehistoric river that no longer exists. Today its slopes are covered with mainly native ash trees.

3. The path narrows to about 20 feet at some points. This is a National Nature Reserve and if you do have a dog with you should keep it on its lead. This ruling is in force to protect the local wildlife, which includes roe deer, foxes, buzzards and the inevitable grey squirrel. You will also notice that some of the trees on your walk have been coppiced, to allow the wild flowers and undergrowth to mature and give shelter to the natural wildlife. At the top of the gorge the path bears round to the right. Follow the footpath signs for the car park.

Look out for the sign that says 'Cliff Edge 50 yards ahead'. It really is worth walking up this part of the track for the short distance indicated, as it brings you out on top of the gorge, with a sheer drop way beneath you. Braver souls might venture to the edge of the cliff to obtain the best of the wonderful view that it offers, but if you do please be very careful. Having taken your fill of the view, return to the signpost, turning right and following the path downhill.

4. This path is circular and will bring you out to where the paths originally separated. Turn left here and follow the footpath back to the village and the inn. The Wookey Hole Caves and Paper Mill are very famous tourist attractions that you may care to take in on your return. You can get further information by telephoning 01749 672243 or visiting the website: http://www.wookey.co.uk.

WELLS

The Kings Head

❧❀❧

Set on the southern side of the Mendips, the walk begins by passing the 14th century Bishop's Palace alongside the cathedral. The unique setting of this lovely building, the residence of the Bishop of Bath and Wells, is a must for any visitor. Unusually, it is surrounded by a wide moat, the home of swans that for generations have rung a bell at the gatehouse when they want to be fed. The first part of the route is very easy going over metalled roads and tarmac paths. The walk then goes uphill across fields before turning right along the wooded ridge. From there it goes down to the base of the hill, returning to Wells along a well-trodden path.

The Kings Head building was reputedly established in 1318 before eventually becoming a public house in 1604. It was listed as a 'new inn' at the time and earned its place in history by being fined ten shillings for charging too much for its ale! I hasten to add that this is not the case now.

The interior is high and spacious and above the bar are some old and interesting wooden beams that have been dated to 1318. For the real ale enthusiasts there are usually six selections available at the pumps at any one time, among them when I was there: Wadworth 6X, Otter Ale,

Taylor's Landlord and Theakston Old Peculier. I had a tasty sandwich made from white bread (a proper Somerset doorstep, two inches thick) with slices of ham from the bone, and a small side salad complete with olive oil dressing. The menu caters for all tastes. Home-made steak and kidney pies, roast pork with apple sauce, chargrilled chicken and dishes of the day were all on offer at the time that I visited.

The pub is dog friendly and more than welcomes responsible owners. You do not need to book to order a meal but it might be wise to do so on a busy Sunday. Telephone: 01749 672141.

- **How to get there:** The A39 and the A371 intersect in the town. The Kings Head is centrally located in the High Street, near to the Bishop's Palace and the cathedral.
- **PARKING:** There are ample public car parking facilities within the city of Wells. It is suggested that you allow yourself a minimum of three hours for the walk and a snack.
- **LENGTH OF THE WALK:** 4 miles. Map: OS Explorer 141 Cheddar Gorge and Mendip Hills West (GR 548456).

THE WALK

1. Leave the pub and turn left along the High Street. Cross over the road on the distinct left-hand bend, passing the remains of the market cross on your right.

2. Ahead is the magnificent archway leading through to the Bishop's Palace. Go through and walk to the right of the palace, following the moat round – look carefully and you will see lots of large stickleback fish and newts. If you are very lucky you might spot the moat's one carp, that has somehow mysteriously appeared. There are also several varieties of waterfowl, as well as the famous white swans. Within the Bishop's Palace itself are found the rising springs from which the name of Wells was derived. The palace is open to the public, but you will have to pay to enter and view the wells in its gardens. For more information visit the website on http://www.bishopspalacewells.co.uk or telephone 01749 678691.

At the far end of the moat you find a splendid large rock that bears the legend 'The Tor 8m'. Walk slightly to the right beyond this rock, crossing over the small stream. Take the left-hand track that has a footpath signpost indicating Dulcote. Follow this path along and up to the road.

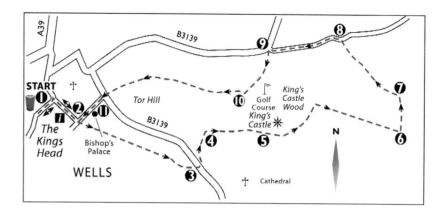

3. Cross over the fairly busy B3139 and go through the kissing gate into the field. Turn immediately left and walk up over the hill towards the gate, keeping the wood to your right. This is quite a steep hill and as you go through the first gateway you will be probably be pleasantly surprised to find evidence of a rich red soil, more usual in Devon than the Mendips.

4. Cross over the field and go just to the right of the pillbox ahead and just to the left of the farmhouse. This pillbox formed one of the Second World War defences that overlooked the Green Line established across the Somerset Levels. As you pass over the stile, turn round and survey the scene behind you. The impressive sight of Glastonbury Tor, far away in the distance and just to your right, holds your attention. The Home Guard who manned this defensive position had this view every day.

Turn right and follow the wide dirt track. Go past the beginning of the golf course on your left and walk on through the wood. The wild dog rose grows in profusion here – the gentle aroma of which wafts through the breeze after a spring shower.

5. After a short distance you will come across a sign on your left that informs you about the role of King's Castle Wood as a nature reserve. As you progress through the wood along the track, you head slightly uphill, and at this point the limestone rock starts to assert itself. You soon pass into the central feature of this walk, a beautiful natural meadow with a profusion of all sorts of wild flowers. From April to October you will find daisies, buttercups, red clover, ox-eye daisies and long forgotten grasses thriving in this natural environment. A profusion of colours, together with several different aromas, vie for your attention and compete with each other to become your favourites.

Keep the wood on your left. Soon you will pass through a wooden farm gate marked 'East Mendip Way'. Go through into the field and follow the wood along until it bears a definite left.

6. Go over the stile at the end of the wood. Keeping the trees on your left-hand side, continue down over the gently sloping hill. Walking down this stretch, and looking at the field on your right, you can see how easy it is to find the materials used to construct the familiar limestone walls so evident in the Mendips.

7. At the point where the wood turns left, you need to angle across to the left-hand edge of the strip of wood to your right. Go down over the steep hill and through the gate, keeping to the left of the two oak trees on your right. In the very narrow field, at the bottom of the hill, turn left. You now need to head towards the church steeple slightly to your right and in the distance.

8. At the minor road, turn left, keeping the golf course on your left. You then join the B3139 again. Turn left here.

9. Almost immediately, by the bus shelter, turn left through the metal kissing gate. Walk along the track until it starts to disappear into the golf course proper. Turn right over the small stream.

10. Keep the sports grounds on your left and the small stream on your right. Follow the grass track all the way along until it becomes metalled; on your left-hand side will be the National Trust woodland area of Tor Hill. As you walk along this track an unusual and unexpected photographic view of Wells Cathedral suddenly appears ahead. Cross straight over the road (the B3139 again) and onto the metalled track.

11. Look out for the mosaic on your left-hand side – created in 2001 by local schoolchildren in order to preserve the local legend of the Worminster Dragon. Keep on walking and soon the Bishop's Palace appears on your right. Follow the moat round and back out to where you left your car

Nr EAST HARPTREE

The Castle of Comfort Inn
✈❦✈

*S*et atop the stunningly beautiful Mendip plateau, the walk starts at
the famous Castle of Comfort Inn. It sets off in a generally easterly
direction, along a high contour line, before turning back to walk
through beautiful Stockhill Wood, passing through a Site of Special
Scientific Interest (SSSI) known as Priddy Mineries. The remains of
lead mining in the form of large ponds and undulating land
characterise the Mendips' industrial legacy. From there an old cattle
drove is followed on the return to the inn.

At first sight, the Castle of Comfort seems to be a rather odd name for an
inn situated in this position. However, we are told that at the time of
notorious Judge Jeffreys in the 17th century it provided refreshments for
condemned prisoners when they were being transported from the
prison at Wells to Gibbets Brow (a little way up the road from the inn),
where they were due to be executed by hanging; some were even drawn
and quartered.

The inn has a very large back garden and on fine days you can eat or drink on the raised wooden decking or choose the picnic benches set aside for this purpose. Inside, there are low ceilings and a blazing fire in winter. Set into the fire surround is a large ammonite, coloured black with time. A regular range of beers and lagers is available and, on the day I visited, there were four real ales and a draft cider on offer. The menu is excellent and varied. On the day I was there, 8 oz steaks with all the trimmings and lamb cutlets were featured, and a traditional roast is always available on Sunday. This is an extremely popular inn with tourists and it is advisable to book a table, particularly on Sunday. Dogs (on leads) are welcome in the Mendip Bar. Telephone: 01761 221321.

- **HOW TO GET THERE:** The village of East Harptree is about 2 miles north-east of the Castle of Comfort, just south of the A368 and West Harptree. The inn lies on the B3134 and stands alone on a long, straight stretch of road. Approaching from Wells, turn off the A39 in the direction of Priddy. A very straight road brings you to the Hunters Lodge Inn on your left. Turn right here along the B3134. At the next crossroads go straight over. The Castle of Comfort is on your left-hand side after about ½ mile.
- **PARKING:** There is ample parking at the inn.
- **LENGTH OF THE WALK:** 6 miles. Map: OS Explorer 141 Cheddar Gorge and Mendip Hills West (GR 543542).

THE WALK

1. Leave the pub and walk straight across the B3134. Cross over into the field just to the left of the postbox by means of an old Mendip limestone stile. Head for the top right-hand corner of the field and the beech trees. Continue into the next field and cross it, keeping the pond on your left. Move into the next field and cross to the far right-hand corner. Go over the stile into the next field and head straight across towards the left-hand edge of the wood ahead of you. In the next field you now need to angle right to the junction of the hedge and the wood. Walk left to the end of the wood and turn right.

2. Walk straight across the field and over the stile next to the metal farm gate. Go forward about 50 yards to the farm track and turn left.

3. You are now well on the Mendips plateau. Follow the track all the way down to where it runs between two sets of limestone walls. Do not go out of this field. Turn right.

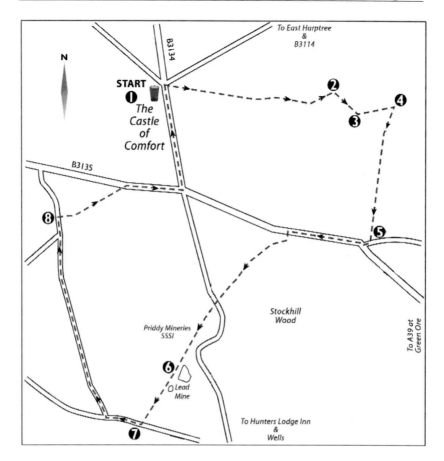

4. Walk along this bridleway, keeping the limestone wall on your left. After a while a line of large trees replaces the wall. Keep these trees on your immediate left and follow them all the way down to a road.

5. At this road, turn right and then right again onto the B3135 towards Priddy. Follow the road up to where it enters the mixed wood. On the left, by the first layby, is a footpath sign. Follow this footpath into Stockhill Wood, a well-known breeding area for long eared owls.

Follow the wide and well-defined gravel track (ignore any other grass tracks diverting off it) along to the first gravel track T-junction. Turn right. At the next T-junction turn right again and walk down the long expanse of track before you. At the next track T-junction turn left and walk down to the road. Cross over into the Priddy Mineries Reserve, where approximately 120 acres of land are set aside as a Site of Special Scientific Interest.

Follow the footpath through the SSSI until you arrive at a large pond on your left. Sometimes you may spot cavers in this pond testing their scuba gear prior to their planned descent into the Mendip caving system. By the Priddy Mineries Reserve signpost, turn right. Continue for about 5 yards towards the boundary wall and turn left.

6. Walk along the well-defined track between the small stream on your left and the wall on your right. Towards the end of this path you will discover the remains of an old lead mine on your left. St Cuthbert's Swallet is located down in the quarry. Here water is collected and piped away to a nearby reservoir. Follow the path out onto a track and go over into the grounds of the bungalow ahead. Turn left in these grounds, keeping the bungalow on your right, and continue into a lane. Follow this down to the road.

7. Turn right along this road and follow it to the next road junction. Turn right into East Water Lane. Follow this long lane up, passing a little caravan site on your left. The metalled road then gives way to an old cattle track known as East Water Drove. Follow this all the way up until it joins a small road. Turn right and pass through the wooden kissing gate into the field.

8. Walk over the brow of the hill, keeping the electric poles on your right. You will see cars on the road going past you on your left. Head towards the metal farm gate in the corner of the copse, passing a swallet hole that the farmer has plugged with limestone rocks to stop the cattle falling into the cave below. Go through this gate onto the road. Turn right. At the crossroads turn left by the old Miners Arms, now a private house, and follow the B3134 back to the Castle of Comfort and your car.

As you go by the entrance to the Castle Farm you pass over the ancient Roman Fosse Way that goes underneath the road you are on and within 50 feet of the farm track entrance. This Roman road leads to Uphill and the Bristol Channel. Its direction is generally north-westerly, passing between the Castle of Comfort and Priddy Circles away to your left.

EAST HARPTREE
The Waldegrave Arms
❧❀❧

This walk begins in the very pretty Mendip village of East Harptree. It takes a gentle route down into Harptree Combe, following along the line of this little known but beautiful miniature version of Cheddar Gorge and passing beneath an impressive feat of engineering, an aqueduct that carries water away to nearby Chew Valley Lake. From there the walk moves up to where proud Richmont Castle once stood, before heading off in a generally south-westerly direction to the Mendip Forest. Here the walker encounters a preserved chimney tower and slimes, the refuse from the local lead mining industry. The route continues across green fields, with a magnificent view of the lake all the way. The return to the village is along quiet country roads via Eastwood Manor and Harptree Court.

The Waldegrave Arms is a beautiful pub set in the heart of the village. Although obviously an old inn, its history is hard to uncover. It was most probably named - along with others in the area - after the local

Waldegrave family, who were granted land around Chewton Mendip in 1553 and lived in Chewton Priory.

The bar is semicircular in shape, but divided into three distinct parts, including two separate eating areas, one of which has a floor made entirely of old bricks. The walls are rough plastered and there is a pervading air of antiquity. The enormous enclosed garden has picnic benches, also a pond containing goldfish and a small fountain to complete the picture.

Food is plentiful and varied. On the day I visited, 12 oz rump steaks, cod and chips and scampi were on offer. There was also a specials board with such delights as lamb rogan josh, moussaka and vegetable bake. Bar snacks, for example the ever-popular sausage, egg and chips, are always available. Two real ales are usually on offer, as well as draught Guinness and a range of other beers and lagers. The pub is extremely dog friendly and welcomes responsible dog owners. Telephone: 01761 221429.

- **How to get there:** Take the A368, which runs between the A38 at Churchill and the A37 west of Bath. In West Harptree take the B3114 and then turn off southwards to reach East Harptree. The pub is in the centre of the village, opposite the church.
- **Parking:** There is ample parking at the inn.
- **Length of the walk:** 6½ miles (a much shorter circuit that just takes you into Harptree Combe is also described). Map: OS Explorer 141 Cheddar Gorge and Mendip Hills West (GR 566509).

The Walk

1. Come out of the pub and turn left, crossing immediately over the road and to the right of the church. Pass through an old Mendip stone stile and walk along a small path. After another Mendip stone stile, go into a field, angling to the right across it. You now get your first of many views of the Chew Valley Lake. Go over a stile and walk down a wide track for about 300 yards.

2. At the old and magnificent oak tree that appears on your right, turn left. Go over a stile and enter the gloriously beautiful Harptree Combe, with its similarities to Cheddar Gorge and Burrington Combe. Not as grand as Cheddar or as deep as Burrington, Harptree has a charm all of its own. Steep limestone walls rise up and offer tantalising glimpses of large nooks and crannies that disappear into the rock face. The small stream gurgles gently by. Walk along the level path, ignoring any small tracks that lead off it. You suddenly reach an unexpected surprise: a large aqueduct appears before you.

This is one of three aqueducts – known as 'the tubes' – on the route down to the reservoir. They are made of wrought iron plates, riveted together to produce an egg-shaped conduit. The Harptree Combe tube is supported by five masonry pillars spaced at 50 foot intervals. As you pass beneath this minor engineering miracle, you encounter deep boreholes that also belong to the Bristol Waterworks Company. On a sunlit day you can peer down and watch the water trickle through below.

Continue until you reach a wooden gate. For those readers who only have time for a short walk (approximately 45 minutes in total), it is possible to return to the village from here: go through the gate and left down the metalled track, turning left again at the road.

3. For other walkers, go right before the wooden gate and follow the track up the hill, still within the woods. At the top you will come across a flat area. Keep to the right at the top of the combe to find Richmont

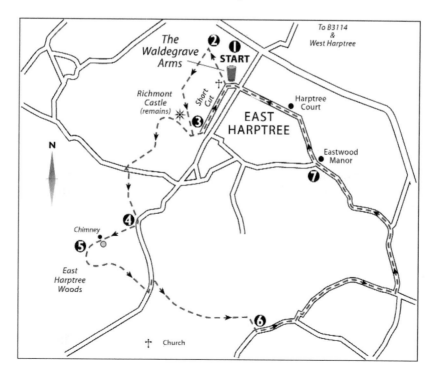

(or Richmonte) Castle, built after the Norman Conquest. For full accounts of its history go to http://www.richmonte.freewire.co.uk/. There is only a small ivy-clad fragment of the wall remaining, but the site is still impressive and indicates that a fine castle once stood here. Explore the mound, noting the castle's defensive position – it must have looked most intimidating from below. The humps and bumps and mysterious holes in the ground are the remains of aggressive calamine digging that once took place here – well before archaeological preservation was thought of. This flat area has a somewhat mystical appeal about it, and if some parts of it seem familiar, it might be because some scenes from the children's serial, *Chronicles of Narnia*, were filmed here.

Walk across the flat area to the line of trees coming from the field on your left. Keeping the field on your left, you will eventually come to a steep slope. If you look carefully, you can take the old pathway between two natural limestone walls and down onto the valley floor. Once on the path below, turn left and follow the small river upstream. At the end of the combe you go over a stile and into a narrow field. Cross this to the left of the house on your right, going over the stile and into the metalled lane. Turn left here and continue for about 100 yards before turning right over the stile and into the next field. Walk up the hill, heading for the top edge of the wood on your right and passing through the corner by the stiles and out into the field beyond. Go straight ahead, walking between a large swallet on your left-hand side and a line of three small oak trees on your right. Walk across the fields straight ahead and you will shortly enter a small lane. Note the views of the reservoir behind you.

4. After about 50 yards, you join another track ahead. On your left is a road. Turn right along this track and walk through the farmyard, keeping the Dutch barn on your right. Pass through the wooden gate and into East Harptree Woods. After about 50 yards, if you look to your right, you will see the glistening slimes, left over from the lead mining days. Another 200 yards and you can see why these slimes exist in the woods. In front of you is all that remains of the Smitham Lead Minery: a large chimney built by Cornishmen in 1867. Walk on the laid out track that goes around the pool. If you pass by in August you will see the large (pink) water lilies at their best. Frogs now own the pond, and an occasional heron can be spotted, patiently waiting for its dinner. Continue all the way along through a plantation of young birch trees until you come to a large track.

5. Turn left here, walking down the track and passing a picnic area on your right. At the metalled road, turn left. Continue for about 200 yards and take the first track right. This leads towards Nettwood Farm. Follow the track along, and, where it bears right to the buildings away to your right, keep walking straight ahead, keeping the row of lovely beech trees on your right. Go through the metal gate at the end of the lane and out into the field. Keeping the hedge on the right, walk straight across the field and over a stile into the next field. Rocky outcrops of limestone push through the grass, whilst away to your left large depressions mark where the ground has dropped into caverns below. In the distance on your left you get an uninterrupted view of Chew Valley Lake. Head towards the right-hand edge of the line of trees in front of you, looking out for the gateway with a metal drinking trough to the right of these trees. Pass through this gateway, keeping the hedge on your left, and cross the field into the lane.

6. Follow this wide and grassy track, Greendown Batch, down to the road. Turn left, following the winding country lane for just over ½ mile. At the next junction, turn left and walk downhill. Pass over a small stream. At the following junction, go left again. About 500 yards later, as you go around a sharp bend to the right, note the water culvert coming out of the ground on your left. This feeds the large pond on your right. Also to your right is Eastwood Manor Farm. A lot of the stone from Richmont Castle was supposed to have been used in its construction, probably explaining why none is left at the castle site itself. Keep walking along this road, passing Eastwood Manor itself. It is interesting to note that on the 1900 OS map of the area, the house now known as Eastwood Manor was just called Eastwood. Perhaps this adds to the general local confusion as to which house was actually constructed out of the castle stones.

7. Very shortly, at the next junction, walk straight ahead, leaving Highfield Lane on your left. The large high-walled garden of Harptree Court follows you along, and it is not until you get almost into the village and opposite Water Street that you catch a glimpse of the large building itself. Keep walking straight ahead and shortly you will pass the school on your left and arrive back at the Waldegrave Arms.

LITTON
The Kings Arms
❧

*T*his route follows the upper reaches of the River Chew to two lovely
reservoirs that are not often visited by walkers. Unlike their bigger
sisters at Blagdon and the Chew Valley, these are small and quiet areas
without watersports. A bankside track leads to a brown trout breeding
area before the walk continues through the hamlet of Sherborne.
Beyond some fishing ponds, the circuit eventually reaches the village
of Chewton Mendip, passing what is arguably the finest example of a
church tower in Somerset. From there the walk returns to the Mendip
plateau, and then descends into Litton once more, taking in distant
views of the Bristol Channel. The surprise of the route is a hidden
water garden quite near the end.

The Kings Arms is a locally well-known and beautiful 15th century inn.
It has two bars, plus a large garden room and a restaurant area. The
spacious garden also has a very good selection of physical activities for
youngsters. There is an air of mystery about the pub. Seven faces of

what is said to be the devil surround the bar. Local legend also has it that Charles II took shelter here when hiding from Oliver Cromwell.

The food is extremely well presented and there is a large choice of meals. On the day that I visited, the blackboard specials included seafood brochettes with a sweet chilli dip and traditional roast beef with Yorkshire pudding. The main menu offered sirloin steak, whole rib racks, chicken curry, salads and various low calorie options. Children are not forgotten either: meals such as chicken nuggets and fish shapes are always available. There are usually three real ales, together with draught Guinness and a range of other beers and lagers. Dogs are welcome, but only in the garden, please. Telephone: 01761 241301.

- **How to get there:** Take the A39, which runs north from Wells to join the A37. At Chewton Mendip turn off on the B3114 towards West Harptree. The King's Arms at Litton is about 2 miles along this road.
- **Parking:** There is ample parking at the inn.
- **Length of the walk:** 6½ miles (a 2 mile circuit from Litton to the reservoirs is also described). Map: OS Explorer 141 Cheddar Gorge and Mendip Hills West and a tiny section on Explorer 142, but you can manage without it (GR 594545).

THE WALK

1. From the front of the pub, turn left and enter the field over a stile between the river and the village hall. Keeping the river on your left, continue to the pump house, then walk around its side and fence and go over the stile onto the road. Turn left and then almost immediately right, through a kissing gate, onto a well-defined track.

Follow this track right around the outside of the reservoir.

2. At the dam that separates the upper from the lower reservoir, you will notice below you netting protecting the brown trout that are being encouraged to breed here. Walk over the small metal bridge and continue down the well-defined footpath. At the bottom of the hill you come level with the lower reservoir on your right.

Continue walking on the footpath and soon you leave the reservoir behind you. Keep the small stream on your right. Enter a very small field, turning immediately right over the stile and back onto the footpath. Follow the track as it widens. Go right over the bridge and then immediately left over the stile. The shallow stream is now on your left. The houses you see belong to the small hamlet of Sherborne. Very soon

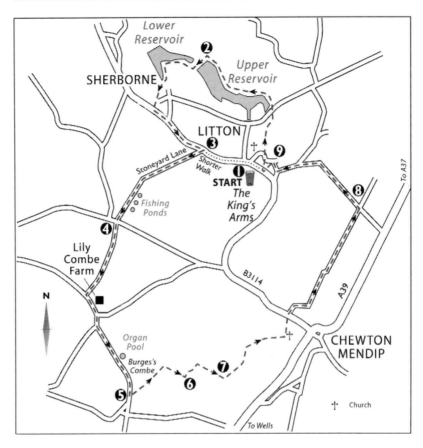

you will come to a building with a metal bridge going back over the stream. On the concrete path someone has painted the points of the compass. Do not go over the stream, but walk round the building and go through the high wooden gate and out onto the track, continuing all the way up to the B3114, where you turn left.

3. Follow this road along to the 'Litton' signpost. If you wish to shorten this walk, just carry on for about another 400 yards and you will arrive back at the Kings Arms.

For the full walk, turn right into a RUPP (Road Used as a Public Path) just before the signpost. A deep ditch runs alongside.

This RUPP soon narrows into a track as it goes through a private wood on your left, eventually coming out to a road. On the way you pass a series of fishing ponds, one of which is set aside for children to fish in.

4. Turn right on this road and then almost immediately left. A signpost points the way to Greendown and Wells. Keep walking along this minor road, passing Lilycombe Farm on your left. At the T-junction, turn left. A signpost points to Wells. At the next junction, walk straight ahead, with cottages on your right. Just past Grove Cottage you will arrive at another junction. Walk straight ahead here.

After about 500 yards, you will find a large pond, Organ Pool, on your right, surrounded by trees. A further 300 yards or so brings you to a mature wood of beech trees on your left and pine trees on your right.

5. After about 100 yards of this wood, you reach a wide bridleway on your left. Follow this, but be careful not to go up the wide track up to the right; instead take the track that goes through the centre of the wood. You will soon notice that you are in a combe. Not as spectacular as Burrington or Harptree, Burges's Combe is nonetheless a pretty area. It has steep sides and a flat bottom with interesting clusters of limestone rocks.

Walk on until you arrive at a wooden bridleway gate. Go out onto the track ahead, turning right. Almost immediately turn left through another wooden bridleway gate and re-enter the combe. Follow the track until you come to an open field. Cross the field, keeping the hedge on your right.

6. Go over the metal farm gate onto a farm track. Turn immediately left and walk back into the wood. The church tower of Chewton Mendip will be away on the horizon to your right. After about 100 yards through the outskirts of the wood, a pedestrian wooden gate on your right takes you into a field. Angle left across this field, keeping the buildings on your right. Go over the stile and onto a track with houses on your right. Walk down to the large barn-type building on your left.

7. Keeping this building on your left, walk along the footpath through the young orchard. Some small ponds will be on your right. Cross over the stile into the next field and follow the hedge, keeping it on your right. Very soon you come to a stile in the hedge on your right. Cross over into the field beyond, angling left and heading directly for the church tower. Go through the kissing gate and into the churchyard.

Before you is what some would say is the finest example of a church tower in the whole of Somerset, and perhaps England. Walk along the church path, passing underneath this magnificent tower and keeping to the path on the left of the churchyard. Continue down to the road (the B3114), where you go straight across and over the river bridge into Kingshill. Walk up the hill, keeping the wood on your left. As you crest the rise there is a magnificent oak tree on your right. Follow this narrow road until you get to a T-junction.

8. Turn left. As you walk along this road you get a glimpse of the upper reaches of the Bristol Channel, with Avonmouth in view on a fine day. Shortly the road starts a deep descent. At the T-junction, turn left. Walk downhill into the outskirts of Litton until you get to the next T-junction. Turn right and continue for about 50 yards, looking out for a house called 'Spring Villa' on your left.

9. You will find a row of houses on your right, with the road sign 'Straight Mead' about halfway up the side of the first house. Opposite this house, keeping Spring Villa on your left, walk to the right of the garage. Go through the wooden gate into what looks like the garden of the house. It is a public footpath. Walk down through the garden, keeping the wall on the right. Follow the footpath round and you will come across a small stream with a pool crossed by a lovely little bridge. Pause here for a moment and you might be lucky enough to spot the blue flash of a kingfisher. Walk up the steps and out onto the road. The King's Arms is just to your right.

GURNEY SLADE
The George Inn
᪥

*T*his short, circular route encompasses the beautiful natural scenery of the eastern end of the Mendips, its lush grassland contrasting sharply with the short grasslands of the west. Starting at a village that is often ignored by motorists, the walk moves gently uphill with a rare view of a large working quarry that can only otherwise be seen from the air. It then passes through a very unusual smallholding of exotic animals before coming upon the jewel in the crown, a delightful hidden valley sheltering a wide and shallow stream, a child's delight, with a Japanese bridge and a waterfall. A mystery suddenly presents itself here: the chiming of a large clock. The walk returns along the rim of the quarry on the way back to the inn.

The George Inn at Gurney Slade is believed to be an original 17th century building. It is decorated in the older bar style and has a good garden at the rear. You are welcomed into the inn through a beautiful porch, bedecked with flowers in summer.

Two real ales are usually on tap, including the local Butcombe Bitter. The inn has a good reputation for food, and on the day I was there dishes ranged from chicken wrapped in bacon and stuffed with Stilton through to smoked haddock and down to the basic ham, egg and chips. Meals can be taken either in the bar or the dining area. Dogs are welcome in the bar or the garden, but not in the food areas. Telephone: 01749 840554.

- **HOW TO GET THERE:** Gurney Slade lies on the A37 to the north of Shepton Mallet. If you are approaching from the south, the George Inn is on the left at the bottom of the hill.
- **PARKING:** There is ample parking at the front of the inn.
- **LENGTH OF THE WALK:** 4 miles. Map: OS Explorer 142 Shepton Mallet and Mendip Hills East (GR 622493).

THE WALK

1. Cross over the A37 in front of the inn, turning slightly right. Walk down the pavement on your left, passing the house 'Ivydene'. Where the pavement meets the road, turn left towards the working quarry. Just before its entrance, turn right up Grunters Lane, bearing right at the track junction and keeping quaintly named 'Albert's Cottage' on your right. Walk up the track for about 5 yards and then go left over the stone stile into the field, angling left towards the junction of the far hedge. Cross over the stile into the next field and walk round its edge, obtaining spectacular views of this quarry, normally hidden from view by the surrounding trees and bushes. Follow the hedge all the way round and go through the metal gate into the next field. Cross this, passing to the left of the ruined farmstead, and walk down the lane.

2. After about 50 yards, at the next track junction, turn right and proceed along the lane, which has several different types of trees: rowan, ash, sweet chestnut and cherry. Where the lane bends to the right, go over the stile and into the field, angling to the right across it and keeping the metal farm gate on your right. Leave the field by the small wooden gate in the corner. In the next field, follow the hedge along on your right, passing a smallholding with an outcrop of grassy limestone. Alpacas can usually be seen grazing the land here – an unusual sight for a Mendip farm field, but these are family pets.

3. Cross into a metalled country lane, turning left and continuing downhill, bearing to the left at all times and noting the view across the

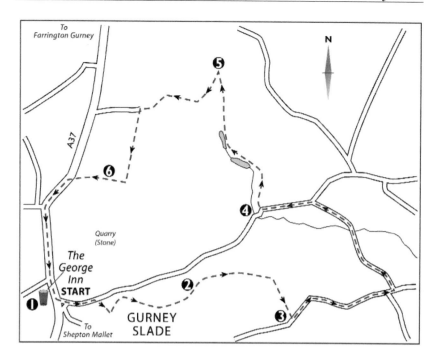

valley as you go. This part of the hill is quaintly called T'other Side the Hill. After a while there is an industrial farm complex on the right. Just before the red postbox set in the wall on your left, turn left towards Gurney Slade. At the bottom of this small valley, the route crosses a hidden stream, given away by a single bridge parapet on the right. Small trout may be viewed here, providing that the approach is made stealthily.

Walk on up this lane, turning left at the next T-junction. Walk through the shady avenue of small trees, turning right and crossing the cattle grid that leads towards Penny Mill Farm. Within 50 yards there is another cattle grid. Go right here and over the stile and into the wood, keeping the stream on your left at all times.

4. This valley is secreted away and nurtures a delightfully old-fashioned mixed wood that opens out into an even older beech wood. The stream is fast, wide and shallow, and a delight for children to explore. After a while you stumble across an unexpected bonus: the grounds of a private house can be made out across the stream, complete with an arched Japanese bridge and a stone statue atop a stepped waterfall. A loud and pretty chiming from a clock can be heard every quarter of an hour, but its source cannot seem to be located. The locals in the pub believe that the chimes are the echoes of the clock at Downside Abbey, some 1½ miles away. You are left to draw your own conclusion.

Follow the valley along, passing large ponds on your left. The ducks are still truly wild along this part of the walk and they fluster in a mêlée as you pass. The wooded area then opens out into an old-fashioned pasture, sheltered from the wind.

5. At the end of this meadow, go through the metal farm gate into the sunken road. Turn left, continuing to the track junction. Turn right and go through the farm gate, following the track round and in front of the farm on your left. After about 100 yards, you go through a metal gate with a stone wall on either side. Turn left here and go over the stile into the field beyond. Keeping the hedge on the right, follow it along and over the stile into the next field, joining a footpath that runs from left to right. Turn right and walk along the hedge, passing the remains of an old brick shed on your right. Over to your left there is a steep drop down into a quarry. When I walked through this field, there were some giant puffballs growing. They have the appearance of large footballs – a temptation for children.

6. Go right over a stile into the next field, following the hedge along on your left until you come to the main A37 road. Go over the stile and follow the grass verge to your left. This leads up to a footpath that skirts the edge of the quarry. Do not take one of the many tracks that go right down to the road, but instead keep on the footpath, with the quarry immediately to your left at all times. Eventually the track leads you down to the road, just before the quarry entrance. Turn right and walk back to the inn.

STRATTON ON THE FOSSE
The Kings Arms
❦

*S*tarting on the Roman Fosse Way itself, this walk passes one of the only two churches in the U.K. named after St Vigor, a French Catholic bishop who died in AD 537. About half of the circuit is over country roads and lanes, and there are lovely views of Downside Abbey. From the pretty village of Holcombe, a walk downhill leads to a now defunct canal. After passing the swiftly flowing upper reaches of the River Mells, a beautiful and little known nature reserve is reached at Nettlebridge. The walk returns to Stratton on the Fosse and world famous Downside Abbey, wherein lie the relics of the last Roman Catholic bishop to be martyred in England.

The Kings Arms is described as Georgian in style and in 1772 was referred to as being 'newly built'. The coat of arms shown on the sign outside is that of George III. The Fosse Way used to form part of the coaching route from Bath to Shepton Mallet and the pub was used as a regular place to change the horses. Outside the inn, high up on the corner of the building and at the junction of the Fosse Way and South Street, can still be seen the 'Ostler's Bell'.

Substantial fare is offered on the bar menu: on the day I visited, it included chilli con carne and ham, egg and chips. The steak and kidney pie is always a popular choice. One real ale is usually available, together with draught Guinness and a range of keg beers and lagers. The pub is dog friendly and welcomes responsible owners but would appreciate advance warning if you intend to take your dog inside. Telephone: 01761 232346.

- **How to get there:** Stratton on the Fosse is on the A367 (the Fosse Way) between Radstock and the A37 north of Shepton Mallet. The King's Arms is opposite Downside Abbey.
- **Parking:** There is parking available at the inn.
- **Length of the walk:** 6 miles. Map: OS Explorer 142 Shepton Mallet and Mendip Hills East (GR 657506).

The Walk

1. Standing on the pavement of the A367 outside the pub, you can see, in both directions, several 'pinch points' on this straight Roman road, just large enough to allow one vehicle through at a time. Modern day traffic calming measures bear a great resemblance to the way in which Roman chariots were also forced to slow down – in those days large stones on each side of the road would have done the trick.

Turn left into South Street. Follow the road round past the Royal British Legion Club and up to the T-junction, where you bear left. The church of St Vigor is on the left, and just opposite it, in the field on your right, you will notice a walled spring with water lilies.

At the next junction, turn right and walk downhill, passing a large pond on your right. Pass the first footpath sign on your left, looking out for the second footpath sign about 100 yards from Little Field Farm, on your left.

2. Go over the stile and cross the field diagonally right, aiming just to the left of the farm buildings. Go straight ahead and over the field stiles until you come to a lane. Cross over, angling left across the field, a little to the right of a large oak tree. Go over the stile into the next field and head towards the building that you see behind the hedge opposite. Cross the stile into the lane.

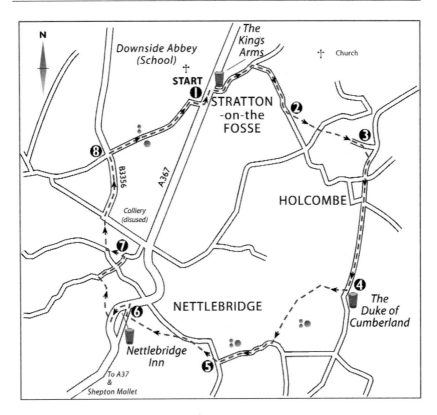

3. At the second footpath sign on your right, marked by a concrete post, walk up the narrow lane to the main road. Turn right. Follow the road through Holcombe, walking downhill and straight ahead, with views of the southern slopes of the Mendips. Pass pretty Tyning Cottages on your left. At the bottom of the hill go over the stile on your right, about 50 yards before you reach the Duke of Cumberland pub.

4. Go straight across the field. You will be walking in a small dip, the remains of what was once part of the Dorset and Somerset Canal. Just before the end of this field you will see a small, double arched canal footbridge on your right. Go just to its left and onto a track. Walk across the bridge and turn left over the stile, continuing straight across the field and through the gateway into the next field. Keeping Edford Wood on your left, follow it all the way round and out onto a small road.

Turn right, keeping the fast and shallow upper reaches of the River Mells on your left. The left-hand side of the wood contains some old oak trees; on the right-hand there is a pine tree plantation. Follow the road along to the sharp right-hand corner. A signpost directs you towards Nettlebridge.

5. Cross over the stile by the signpost and into the field. Walk up the track to your right, keeping the wood on your left. Cross the field, heading to the left of the farm buildings. Join the road here and turn immediately left. After about 20 yards, go through the metal farm gate onto a track, continuing for about another 20 yards before you angle slightly left across the field to a stile. Cross over into the next field, heading for the stile straight ahead. Follow the footpath along. The overhead electric lines will lead you through a metal gate and onto a road. Turn right uphill for about 200 yards, before rejoining the A367 and turning left downhill. The Nettlebridge Inn is on your left.

6. About 100 yards along on the right, turn into the signed footpath and walk along the lane to the end. You now enter the wonderful Cockles Fields Nature Reserve. The track goes uphill or keeps to the bottom of the hill, with the marshy area on your right. Take the bottom track, but note the erratic earthworks, mounds and dips on your left, the remains of the earliest recorded coal mining activities of the Mendips. There is speculation that the Romans may also have mined here, the open pits being only some 200 yards from the Fosse Way. The whole area is now just fields.

The nature reserve is approximately 11½ acres in area and managed by the Somerset Wildlife Trust. Because of this the meadowland is very natural and encourages a variety of wildlife. At the end of the boggy area, cross over the stile into the next field, angling left but to the right of the house on your left. Go out onto a lane. Turn right and walk up to the crossroads. Go straight across and start walking uphill towards the wood, keeping the high stone wall on your right.

7. About halfway up the hill, and opposite Benter Coach House on the right, go left over the stile and into the field. Keep the wood on your right and walk along the high track, with a beautiful view across the valley, particularly taking in the nature reserve, where you can now easily see the remains of the coal mining pits. Go through the narrow gateway into the next field, keeping the house with the small wooden gate on your left. After about 50 yards go right into the wood over the stile, just where the electric lines are. Walk up through the strip of wood along the path and out into a field. There are some caves in these woods somewhere. One of them was excavated by a monk from Downside Abbey in 1905 and the skeletons of a male and female were discovered, together with Bronze Age artefacts.

As the path leaves the wood, cross diagonally left across the field and just to the right of the house that appears to your left. Go over the stile onto the road. Follow the larger road straight ahead, passing Mendip View and Old Rock Farm on your right. There used to be an extensive colliery system here, still marked as such on the OS map, although now replaced by a more modern business unit.

8. At the crossroads, go right and follow the road (Green Lane) signposted to Stratton on Fosse, passing a large ornamental pond on your right. Continue through a lovely avenue of sweet chestnut and beech trees and reach the school playing fields on your left. Where the road bends to the right, a beautiful view to Downside Abbey and School opens out before you, best experienced by walking up the public bridleway on your left for about 50 yards. The 166 foot tower has a large bell called the 'Great Bede' that rings out every day to announce the services. The church contains the earthly remains of St Oliver Plunkett, the Roman Catholic Bishop of Armagh who was executed at Tyburn in 1681.

The monks run a shop that is open to the public for the purchase of books: information from books@downside.co.uk or telephone 01761 235134. The Abbey church is normally open until early evening, closing between 1 and 2 pm. There is no charge. For information about the abbey itself and the Benedictine order, visit the website: downsideabbey.co.uk.

Follow the road back to the main Fosse Way, turning left and passing the main entrance to Downside Abbey on your left. The pub is on the right. The church and bookshop are at the end of Abbey Road, approximately 500 yards from the pub.

WALK 16
STOKE ST MICHAEL
The Knatchbull Arms
❧

Set at the eastern end of the Mendips, the walk begins at the well-known Knatchbull Arms and soon visits the entrance to a cave before moving up and over the Mendips. A gentle stroll down a slight slope leads into the valley of Stoke Bottom, where a village once existed. Before returning to the inn, the trail takes the walker through a beautiful valley where wild watercress abounds next to a babbling brook. Stoke St Michael stands on St Michael's ley line that pre-dates Christianity, adding a sense of mystery to this lovely walk.

The Knatchbull Arms stands in the heart of the village at the crossroads – a place full of character and a fine example of what a traditional village pub should be. It is named after the Knatchbull family, and it is their ancient coat of arms that is proudly displayed on the pub signboard. There is also has a well-kept secret. During the Second World War the pub was used for a top-secret meeting prior to D-Day by a host of American generals. Some older residents can still recall an extraordinary number of staff cars in the village on that particular day. It is known that General Montgomery was based nearby at Frome during this period.

When I visited, the pub had two real ales on offer, Old Peculier and Oakhill Bitter, also Thatcher's draught cider on tap. On the day that I was there food was not available, just crisps and nuts. However, the landlord is happy for you to bring your own sandwiches to eat whilst you have a pint of beer or something else. There are some picnic benches provided outside that the walker can use. The pub is a very dog friendly and welcomes responsible owners. Telephone: 01749 840354.

If you are walking on a Sunday and want a cooked lunch, there is a great restaurant named Bentley's literally just around the corner from the pub. It has an excellent reputation locally and is fast becoming one of the best-kept secrets of the Mendips. Although not open at lunchtime on other days, Bentley's is willing to consider opening especially for you if you have a party of ten or more. Telephone: 01749 841134.

- **How to get there:** Just north-east of its junction with the A37, turn eastwards off the A367 at Oakhill, by the Oakhill Inn. Continue into Stoke St Michael. The pub is on the left-hand side in the centre of the village.
- **Parking:** There is ample parking behind the pub.
- **Length of the walk:** 5 miles. Map: OS Explorer 142 Shepton Mallet and Mendip Hills East (GR 664469).

The Walk

1. Leave the pub and turn left into Church Street. On your right is the village green, covering what was once the ancient village pond. Note the beautiful gateway erected as the village's commemoration of the millennium year, also on your right. Walk on up the road and at the church of St Michael and all Angels turn right. This church was completely demolished in 1838, with the exception of the tower, and rebuilt on a larger scale. Follow the lane until you come to a weighbridge on your left. Note this point, as the walk will return to this spot after visiting the cave.

2. Walk straight ahead, keeping the stream on your right. Soon you will pass a disused quarry on your left. Old quarry machinery stands forlornly rusting away, a remnant of the time when their great power was responsible for the movement of thousands of tons of earth and rocks. The path then dips down to your right. Here the rushing stream disappears into a cave, locally called Slocker Hole. Please do not attempt

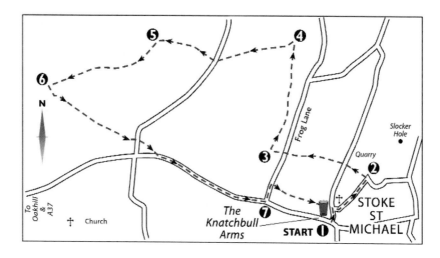

to enter – the published warnings on how to get help for cavers indicate that even the professionals can find themselves in difficulties.

When you have satisfied your curiosity, return to the weighbridge. You now need to turn right, crossing the field straight ahead and walking up the small ridge. Cross over the road and into the field beyond by means of the stile. Continue over the next field, keeping the school playing fields on your left. Go over the metalled lane and into the field. Walk straight on downhill, with the high and wide hedge on your right.

3. After about 50 yards, turn immediately right and walk downhill for 10 yards or so to the bottom of the valley, keeping the ruined building and small quarry on your left. Turn right again and walk down the hill and into the little valley running north. The track carries on downhill and then turns definitely to the right and uphill, but you need to go straight ahead and on through the wood, towards the farm ahead.

4. At the farm, turn left. Keeping the hedge on the right, follow it to the end of the field. Pass out of this field and onto a track. Turn left here, following the track along for about 10 yards and then going out into a field, with the hedge on the right. Walk straight across the fields, keeping the wood on the left and the hedge on the right. At the road, go straight across and into the field. Keep the wood on your left and follow the footpath round and into the wood immediately in front of you.

5. By the ruined building, take the left-hand footpath that directs you towards Oakhill. The path follows the line of a small stream down through a lovely valley. Stop for a moment and listen carefully to the babbling brook and drink in the silence and majesty of the place. The recent remains of industry in the form of old watercress beds can also still be seen here. Limestone rocks spring unexpectedly from the ground, the harshness of their colour hidden from view by a deep rich covering of green moss. In places water gushes out from small caves, joining the stream. Elsewhere it disappears unexpectedly into small swallets (places where water from a surface stream sinks underground).

6. Where the footpath splits into three, follow the left-hand path. Walk up the side of the steeply wooded valley, following the line of a moss-covered limestone wall on your right. Cross out of the wood into the field beyond. Go over the fields, keeping the hedge on your left all the way, and you will eventually come out into a small metalled lane. Cross over the lane and into the next field, angling right to the first house on your right. At the road, turn left and pass a smallholding on your right.

7. At the next road junction, just before the 30 mph sign, turn left down the lane. Before the playground sign, turn right over a small stile and go into the sports field. Cross the field and exit just to the left of the large and magnificent ash tree. Follow the road round until you happen upon a large green area with a clump of trees ahead of you. About halfway along this green area, turn right and follow the footpath towards Tower Close. Continue down to the church and return to where you parked your car.

WALK 17
CRANMORE
The Strode Arms
❧❦❧

Set on the far southern slopes of the Mendips, this circuit begins at the pretty village of Cranmore. Leaving the pub and the village pond behind, the route continues by way of the East Somerset Steam Railway – and as the walk progresses you may hear the whistle and see the smoke of the steam engine as it completes one of its trips. An ancient tithe barn, St Aldhem's Well and the old Fosse Way are visited en route, with the opportunity of actually walking up a now traffic-free section of this world famous road.

Some of the building that is now the pub dates back to the 14th century. It was originally a row of cottages and then a farm before eventually becoming an inn. The signboard shows the coat of arms of the Strode family, who owned the extensive South Hill Estate until 1896.

A spacious dining area is set aside for meals. There is also a front patio and a rear garden. Should the weather be cold, there is an outstanding open fireplace in the bar area.

The food is well presented and the menu comprehensive. On the day I visited, chicken, bacon and avocado salad, chicken pasta, sausages and squeak, smoked trout and a variety of steaks were among the dishes available. There is also a 'Fish Special' blackboard and a special children's menu. The pub is well used to walkers and provides a good and wholesome choice of sandwiches. Three or four real ales are usually on offer, together with draught Guinness and a range of other beers and lagers. The pub is dog friendly. Telephone: 01749 880450.

- **How to get there:** Take the A361 Shepton Mallet to Frome road, turning off south-east into the village of Cranmore. The way to the pub is well signposted.
- **Parking:** There is ample parking at the inn.
- **Length of the walk:** 6½ miles. Map: OS Explorer 142 Shepton Mallet and Mendip Hills East (GR 668432).

The Walk

1. Go out of the pub and turn right, leaving the pretty village pond on your left. Walk up to the T-junction and turn left. Walk down towards the East Somerset Railway, turning right up the lane and passing through the 'No Entry' signs. Keep the line on your left.

Continue up this metalled lane, ignoring any signs. At the end of the track, walk on towards the house that has a stone number '186' incorporated into its wall. Turn immediately right behind the ruined building and cross over the stile into the field. Walk along the side of the wood until it bears sharp left. At this point, angle right across the field, to the left of the clump of trees. At the crossroads, go straight over.

2. Turn immediately left into the field behind the bus shelter with the name 'Cranmore Piers'. Cross the sports ground about 100 yards to the left of its buildings, going over the stile and into the large field behind. Keeping the hedge on your right, follow it to a stile and walk straight across the fields, following the line of the footpath, until you enter another sports ground with a house away on your left. Go over the stone stile into a field, crossing diagonally right to a metal gate next to a house. Follow the very short track out to the metalled road and turn left.

3. Continue,with a wood on your right, and you will meet a large gritted track on your right that goes through the wood. Follow this all the way down until you reach the lip of a major quarry.

79

4. Turn left on the footpath. Keep the quarry away to your right and slightly behind you. Follow the edge of the wood to come out into a narrow but long field. Turn right, walking underneath and following the ridge of earth that has been thrown up by the quarry company. Cross just to the left of the double electric poles at the far end of the field and go over the stile onto the A361 road. Turn right here and walk into Doulting. At the crossroads, go left down the road next to the Abbey Barn Inn. In about 200 yards, you will get a fine view of the 15th century tithe barn. Built of the local Doulting stone, it is well worth the slight diversion to see it. Once you have had your fill of this beautiful building, return to the crossroads and go straight over, keeping the post box on your left. Walk down the street displaying the dead end signs. At the church, turn right and walk down the footpath. At the end of the path you come out into a little street near The Old Bell House. Turn left here and, keeping the house on your right, walk down the hill.

On your left you will see water coming out from beneath a wall. This is St Aldhelm's Well and the source of the River Sheppey.

5. Just below the well, walk to the right of the wooden gate and down a small track, signposted towards Bodden Cross. There is a large pond on the left. At the end of the track, go over the stile and into a field, turning left. Follow the line of the footpath down the valley, keeping the

The 15th century tithe barn at Doulting

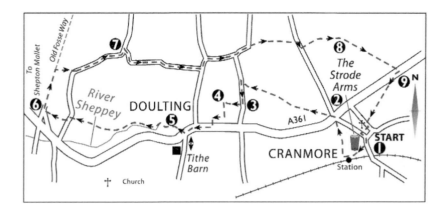

large pond and the River Sheppey on your left. As the river drops down, the footpath gradually rises, but it is still an easy path to follow. Eventually you meet a small lane, where you go left.

Walk down the lane for about 50 yards and turn right over the stile into the field. Head towards the right-hand edge of the buildings in front of you and go out onto a potholed metalled track.

6. At this track, turn right. This is the old Fosse Way. Walk on up the hill, noting away to your left the long-defunct Somerset and Dorset Railway's Charlton Viaduct, with its amazing 27 arches.

Walk on up the Fosse Way to a gas pumping station on your left. Turn right here into the field and walk towards a house in the distance. Some 200 yards later, turn right and up the bank and across to a metal farm gate. Walk out onto the lane. Turn left here and continue up the slight hill.

7. At the next road junction, turn right. Immediately on your right are the remains of an ancient cross. Walk on down this minor road, keeping Pitts Wood on your right and a large pond on your left. At the next junction, turn left. Ignore any roads going off this road and follow it straight ahead. Pass Hither Broadpool Farm on your left. Very soon the road will bend sharply to the left. Go onto the farm track that leads to Yonder Broadpool Farm. Go over the railed metal stile that is immediately to your left, turning right. Keeping the farm track on your right, follow it through the field and past the farm. Walk over the fields, keeping Burnthouse Farm on your right. Climb the stile into the road ahead. Cross this road, going just to the right of the bungalow about 50 yards away. Follow the footpath sign and walk down the narrow track and out into the fields beyond. Keeping the hedge on the left, come to a metalled lane. Cross over this lane and carry on up the track.

8. Where it definitely bends to the left, walk straight ahead on the lines of an old track. Keep the small wooded area on your left. Away to your left in the distance, you will see the Victorian folly known as Cranmore Tower. Walk through a metal gate into the field beyond, angling right, down towards a small ash tree growing in roughly the middle of the line of the hedge in front of you. Go through the gap and into the field beyond, still angling downhill and just to the right of the chapel you can see ahead. Go out through the wooden kissing gate onto the main road.

9. Turn right, walking across the bridge of a small stream. Go immediately left through the wooden kissing gate and into the field beyond. Cross to the right of the furthest oak tree that is growing by itself in the field. As you crest the rise, Cranmore's church tower will come into view. Head for the gateway in the hedge, just to the right of the tower. Go through a wooden kissing gate and into the next field. Still head for the church tower as you cross this field, eventually leaving it by way of a metal kissing gate. Follow the small street to its end, turning left and then right into the churchyard. Keeping the church on the right, walk through the churchyard and out the other side. Go down the road and up to the junction. Turn left. Go down the road and then turn left again to the Strode Arms.

MELLS

The Talbot Inn

❧

*T*he village of Mells is a most beautiful and ancient place. The walk
starts by visiting the grave of a world famous poet. From there the
route moves along the swiftly flowing Mells Stream and into the lovely
Wadbury Valley, a narrow and exciting place guarded by an ancient
hill fort. Moving past another hill fort, the aptly named Murder Combe
is reached before dropping down into Nunney Combe. After a brief
visit to Nunney Castle, the walk moves on to Chantry, before returning
to Mells.

The Talbot Inn has retained its 15th century character and boasts an old
tithe barn that is now the main bar. Old oak beams provide a prominent
reminder of the past, whilst the walls are traditionally painted with an
old-fashioned white limewash. There is also an enclosed rear garden
with hops and kiwi plants growing in profusion.

   The inn has an award-winning restaurant and the food served is of a
high standard. The menu contains such items as Devon mussels cooked

in white wine, chargrilled sirloin steak with celeriac and wild mushrooms and local ham with free-range eggs and fries. A variety of freshly prepared sandwiches is also available. Two real ales are usually on offer, together with draught Guinness and a range of other beers and lagers. Dogs are welcome in the courtyard or garden if they are on a lead.

The inn has a website: www.talbotinn.com. Telephone: 01373 812254.

- **How to get there:** Turn northwards off the A361 between Shepton Mallet and Frome, following the signs for Mells.
- **Parking:** There is limited parking at the inn but plenty around the village.
- **Length of the walk:** 7½ miles. Map: OS Explorer 142 Shepton Mallet and Mendip Hills East (GR 727492).

The Walk

1. Leave the inn and turn left along the main street. Take an immediate turning left towards the church. Go through the gates of St Andrew's, passing to the right of the church and following the path round. Turn right across the churchyard, past a grave shaped like a casket. Turn left at the next row of graves. A stone grave slab lying flat on the ground is ahead. Two headstones back towards you from this stone is the grave of the poet, Siegfried Loraine Sassoon, who died in 1967.

The headstone on the grave of Siegfried Sassoon

After visiting the grave, return to the main village street and turn left. Just before the war memorial note the fine old tithe barn on your right, now part of a garden centre. Continue down the hill, ignoring the turning to Buckland Dinham. Pass the post office on your left. On your right, take note of the large pool, part of the Mells Stream, between the two old

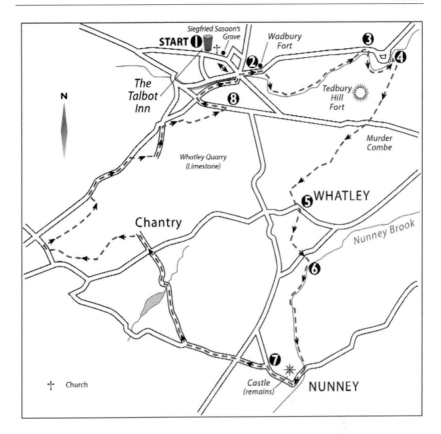

bridges. The walk returns to this spot later. Take the road that is signposted to Great Elm, keeping the river on your right. As you leave the village you come to a layby on your right.

2. Go right here along the bridleway and through the beautiful wooded Wadbury Valley. Walk down the track, with the Mells Stream on your right, passing through the derelict remains of Fussel's Iron Work factory.

The track then becomes metalled. After about 100 yards turn off right, following the footpath sign to Frome.

3. At the steel bridge, cross the river and now keep it on your left.

4. Walk straight ahead on the footpath, keeping the stream and railway line on your left. The track then moves away from this stream a little and hits a small trail crossing to the front. Take the left-hand track and you will find yourself back at the stream. Follow the footpath and cross the private railway line that carries limestone from Whatley Quarry to Frome.

Walk up the combe to the top. Another footpath joins from the left. Ignore this, turning right along the path. Soon the footpath joins a small road. Turn left for about 50 feet and then go right over a stile into a field. Continue across the fields over stiles until you come to a long field with a church spire in the distance. Walk along the right-hand hedge and up to the corner. Cross the stile into the next field and then angle briefly left across to the metal farm gate. At this gate you need to angle left again and cross the stile into a lane. Walk along the lane to the road, where you continue straight ahead.

5. At the Sun Inn turn right along the lane. Go over the stile and into the field next to the house 'Moon Out'. Walk diagonally left, ignoring the stile across the field next to the farm buildings. Walk down the hill towards the line of trees, with the hedge and road on your right. Head to the right of the small pond and drinking trough, passing through a kissing gate into the next field. Turn immediately left, walking down the hill with the hedge on your left. There is a small stream – usually dry in the summer months – on your left behind the hedge. Leave the field and cross over a narrow metalled road, heading down the well-made track. Cross over the stream by the large bridge.

6. Once over the bridge, turn right and walk along Nunney Combe. Follow the footpath through a small wood, with a stream on your right, and eventually come out onto a metalled road. Walk straight on, keeping the river on your right. Enter Nunney, with Fulwell Lane joining from the left. Turn right at the first T-junction. The old market cross is on your right. At this point the river is wide, with metal stools along the riverbank. Shortly you will see a pub sign that runs completely across the road. Just before this, turn right over the river footbridge and into the remains of Nunney Castle, constructed in 1373 in a French style. During the Civil War it was attacked and badly damaged by the Roundheads, leaving it very much as you find it now. Once you have had your fill of this excellent example of a castle, continue up the road and turn right up Castle Hill.

7. Turn left at the very next junction. Follow the road along to the crossroads, going straight over. There is a large wood away to your right. At the next T-junction turn right into a small lane. There is a signpost at this point that says 'weight limit ½m ahead'. Follow the lane, and on your left-hand side is a large pond. It was constructed by Fussel's to build up a head of water for an iron factory, and is now a very attractive feature. Walk on up the small hill and you will pass a high stone wall with a wooden gateway on your right – the site of the former iron works.

Go straight over at the crossroads, continuing down the bridleway. The metalled road then runs out at limestone-producing Whatley Quarry. Although the OS map shows the route going ahead at this point, this is not possible because of quarrying; the bridleway therefore takes you to the left here. Follow it along the well-marked track, keeping the quarry on your right. After ½ mile or so the route passes through a small wood, then turns right at the T-junction and heads towards a farm in the distance, called Finger Farm. This lane has lots of wooden gates, each marked with a sign: 'Please leave the gate as you find it'.

Walk on up to the farm, through the wooden gates and around the perimeter of the farm, and then back on to a well defined track once more. At this point there is a road immediately on your left, on the other side of the hedge, but our track goes off to the right. Walk down this track and through the wood, eventually coming out onto the metalled lane that you were on much earlier. Turn left and walk along the lane, passing Mells Green Farm on the right. Just before the crossroads, turn right over a stile into a field and walk across it, keeping the hedge on your right. Go over the stile onto a small metalled lane. Follow this along to the house, going up a track to its right. Cross a stile into another field, angling left across it but to the right of the electric pole. Go out into the next long field and continue beside the line of electric poles; then go over a stile and out onto the road.

8. Turn left and walk down the hill into Mells, turning right at the crossroads. Soon you arrive back at the large pool that you passed on your way out. At the crossroads you will find the post office again. Take the next left turn and return to your car.

WELLOW
The Fox and Badger

❧

*S*et *on the northern edge of the Mendips, the beautiful village of Wellow once had its own railway line, and the route passes two remaining magnificently arched bridges. From there the walk moves along the valley floor of the clear Wellow Brook before heading gently uphill to a fine example of a chambered long barrow, which can be entered – a small torch is recommended. Continuing along the Wellow Valley, Second World War anti-tank defences, still in their original position, can be seen. Beyond Peasdown St John, the walk traces the ridge line of another lovely valley, with excellent views towards Bath, and then passes the site of a Roman villa before returning to the Fox and Badger.*

This pub was formerly the New Inn. In 1958 the villagers were tired of the lack of originality and decided to rename it. Two suggestions emerged as favourites: one was the Fox and the other the Badger. Arguments raged. One morning the landlord found a dead badger on one side of the door and a dead fox on the other. Since then the pub has been known as the Fox and Badger – the only one in the country with this name. The whole place has an old-time feel to it, which is not surprising, as there has been a building here since the 16th century, although no one actually knows when it became a pub. There are two bars, one the public bar and the other a non-smoking dining room.

On the day I was there, the menu offered chicken and avocado, Somerset pork and a variety of steaks. The pub is renowned for its ploughman's lunches, which feature farmhouse cheeses. Four real ales are usually available, alongside traditional Cheddar cider, Guinness and a range of cask bitters and lagers. Dogs are welcome, but in the bar only. Further information is on the website: www.foxandbadger.co.uk. Telephone: 01225 832293.

- **How to get there:** Take the A367 between Radstock and Bath. Turn eastwards off the Peasedown St John bypass on the road signposted to Wellow.
- **Parking:** There is some parking at the inn but ample free parking in the nearby car park.
- **Length of the walk:** 6 miles. Map: OS Explorer 142 Shepton Mallet and Mendip Hills East (GR 739582).

THE WALK

1. Leave the pub and turn right along the main village road. Go down the small, sharp descent next to the church and look out for a footpath sign on your right. This directs you through a wooden gate next to Brook Lodge. Walk on down the tarmac path in front of this house until you arrive at another gate. The railway line once ran between this and the gate opposite. Both are original, and the nearest one threatens the walker with a dire punishment of 'a penalty not exceeding 40 shillings' for not closing the gates behind them.

Walk downhill, pausing to glance behind to observe the splendid five-arched bridge that still spans the small road. This bridge used to carry the Somerset and Dorset Line through the Wellow Valley. Continue down the hill and over the stile into the field beyond.

2. About 50 yards, in the hedge on your right, you will find a stile going over to the next field. Go right and follow the line of the valley, keeping the Wellow Brook on your left. Cross over a stile onto a small road, turning left. There before you is a pedestrian bridge that crosses the river, or if you prefer you can walk across the ford. Walk on up the road, and after about 100 yards turn right at the track junction.

3. About 100 yards later, the road bends boldly to the left. Go straight ahead and up the farm track, a bridleway. Just before you crest the rise, you will see a burial mound way down to your right. Do not cross the field here but carry straight on up the track. As the track starts to go slightly downhill, turn left through the wooden gate into the field. Keep the hedge immediately on your right and start to walk downhill again. Very shortly you will come to a stile on your right. A footpath marker indicates the Stoney Littleton chambered long barrow. The walk now diverts slightly to visit the barrow and then returns to this point.

4. Go over the stile and walk along the field, keeping the hedge – and the barrow – on your right. Go over the next stile and walk up to the barrow. This beautiful monument is maintained by English Heritage and is believed to be over 5,000 years old. The tunnels are very low (probably about 4 feet high in places) and the visitor will have to stoop quite considerably to scrabble along inside – but the experience is without parallel.

Return to point 4 (see map) to carry on the walk. From this junction, walk diagonally right across the field towards the gateway in the right-hand corner, descending as you go. Keep the hedge and river on your right.

5. Go through the metal bridleway gate and walk across the field towards Manor Farm. At the farm, go through the gate and out onto the track beyond. Follow this to the minor road, where you turn right and pass the village sign of Stoney Littleton. Go over the river bridge and walk up the road, passing a turning on your right. Just beyond it, go over the stile on your left and into the field. Walk up the river valley, keeping Wellow Brook on your left. Go to the end of this long and narrow field and cross over another stile, into a lovely little lane, which you follow up to a minor road. Turn left and pass over the river bridge. Note the pyramid-shaped concrete anti-tank defences left over from the Second World War, placed here to stop enemy tanks crossing the river at this point if the bridge were blown up. Follow this narrow road on up the hill.

6. When you come to two houses, one either side of the road, turn right and follow the footpath to the right of the house that is immediately on

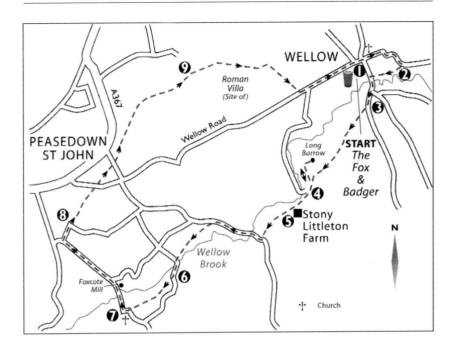

your right. The far end of the footpath has been grubbed away and you now have to walk through what appears to be the garden of the house. Go over the stile into the field beyond and cross it, keeping the electric poles on your left. Passing over the stile into the second field, head just to the left of where the electric lines go over a hedge in front of you. Enter the next field over the stile and walk directly towards the house, keeping the hedge on the left. Go over the metal gate into the lane. You need to go right here, but you might want to make a small detour to your left to look at Foxcote's beautiful little church – St James the Less – set in a lovely calm and secluded spot, with old houses on both sides.

7. To continue, descend steeply into the valley, passing Foxcote Mill on your right. You will see lying against the wall the remains of a grinding wheel once used for turning corn into flour. The mill is now a private house. Walk on over the river bridge to find another arched railway bridge standing alone there, part of the old S&D line. Continue along the road and at the crossroads walk straight up and over the hill, passing some young horse chestnut trees. At the next junction, turn right and walk down the hill, following the road sign for Shoscombe. After about

300 yards, you will arrive at a sharp right-hand bend. Do not go around this bend but walk straight up the track in front of you.

8. Go through the metal gate and take the track immediately on your right. Follow this all the way along to the road. Cross the road and go over the stile into the field. Cross the field, keeping the hedge on your right, to meet another small road. Cross over the road but go through the furthest right-hand gate and into the field. Walk along the bridleway across the fields, keeping the hedge on your left. After a while the open track goes into an enclosed track, with a footpath running from left to right in front of you. Walk straight ahead, noting the lovely views to your left across the valley and towards Bath. Continue until you meet a large track running from left to right. A Dutch barn marks the spot.

9. Go right. After about 300 yards, cross over the wooden stile into the large field on your right, with a wood in the dip away down to your right. In the field behind the wood and to the right are the earth-covered remains of a well-preserved Roman villa. You now need to head diagonally down this field. Walk to the left of the wood and aim just above the far right-hand corner of the field. Go over the wooden stile and walk across to the hedge ahead. Pass through the metal pedestrian gate into the next field. Walk along, keeping the hedge on your left all the way, and continue round the field, heading towards the barn. Go through the metal gate and out into the road. Turn left here and you are back in Wellow.

OLDFORD
The Ship
❧

This short and easygoing route is at the very eastern end of the Mendips, starting in the hamlet of Oldford on the outskirts of Frome. It encompasses country lanes, the River Frome, a scenic golf course and a fine old country mansion built in 1858. The surprise of the circuit is the small church tucked away on an island in Orchardleigh Lake. The walk then follows the southern edge of the lake until meeting a Victorian-built temple and an ironwork bridge and returning to the starting point.

The Ship is a most unlikely name for a pub set firmly in the countryside. It is assumed to be a 17th century building and has two iron hoops in its eastern wall, allowing horses to be tied there. These are plainly visible to the visitor in Iron Mill Lane, which is named after the nearby mill. The pub is unusual amongst Mendip hostelries in that it still has a ninepin skittle alley that is in regular use.

At the back of the pub is a large and sheltered garden, put down mostly as lawn, a pleasant place to be on fine days. Alternatively one can sit at the front of the inn, set back from the road, and watch the world pass by.

There is a dining area just off the bar. The menu is comprehensive and the portions are generous. On the day I visited, the dishes included chicken and beef curries and scampi. There was also a 'Steak Specials' board, together with 'Snack Specials'. Two real ales are usually on offer, also draught Guinness and a range of other beers and lagers. The pub is dog friendly and welcomes responsible dog owners in the garden. Telephone: 01373 462043.

- **HOW TO GET THERE:** Turn off the A361 north-east of Frome onto the B3090, signed for Oldford and Frome. The pub is in the centre of the village.
- **PARKING:** There is ample parking at the inn.
- **LENGTH OF THE WALK:** 4 miles. Map: OS Explorer 141 Shepton Mallet and Mendip Hills East (GR 787502).

THE WALK

1. Come out of the pub, down the steps and into the car park, turning left. Cross Iron Mill Lane and go through a stone stile. Walk to the right of Oldford Farm, through the landscaped gardens, and to the right of the ponds. Cross over the stile into the minor road.

2. Turn left on this road. Walk past the modern industrial complex – a milk processing plant – and over the road bridge, beneath which the River Frome passes, wide and fast flowing. Follow this lovely level lane along, ignoring the first obvious footpath on your left-hand side. The River Frome bends in towards the road from the right, and at the small bridge and cottage to your right, and the obvious weir, turn left over the stile. Walk up this little bit of rough ground, keeping the small stream on your right. Quite soon you will find the golf course on your left-hand side. Walk up to the metalled track that crosses in front of you. The tee for the 13th hole is immediately on your left, whilst a curious horseshoe-shaped bridge is on your right. This track then leads up to an even odder building, called Gloucester Lodge. Walk straight ahead over the track and up to a dirt track. Turn left here and follow the footpath back down to the metalled track that you have just left.

3. Turn right. Follow the track along and you walk through the beautifully sculptured golf course contained within the 800 acres of

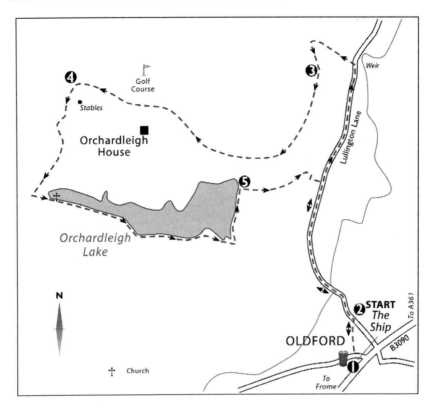

Orchardleigh Park. It is an active course, so please be on the look out for players as they drive their shots, as even the best golfers can sometimes slice their shots. Keep on this track and follow it through the park. Mature oak and horse chestnut trees indicate the age of the area you are walking through. Shortly you will pass an old building called Temple Lodge, on your right. To your left, exceptionally fine views of Orchardleigh Lake open up. The lake is quite big, occupying an area of approximately 28 acres. Keep going along this fairly level and easy metalled track. Very soon you will be passing the Orchardleigh Golf Clubhouse on your right, and about 300 yards later the Grade II listed Orchardleigh House will be on your left. This was built for the Duckworth family and stayed with them until the last male Duckworth died in 1986. Keep walking on until you come to a stable block on your left, with a typical arched entrance way into the yard itself.

4. Just after the stable block, take the track left. A signpost will point the

way towards the church. Follow the track downhill until you come to Church Lodge on your right. The track then bends around to the left, passing some ruins on your left. There in front of you is an ancient church set upon an island. Walk over the bridge and onto the island – a beautifully quiet and serene place. Mallard and teal ducks will probably swim towards you, anticipating a feed of some sort. The last resting places of the Duckworth family can be seen next to the lake. When you have had your fill of this peaceful scene, leave the island and walk round to the right-hand side along a plainly marked track, with the water on your left. Soon you will come to a point where there is a large dam on your left. Do not go over this dam, but walk along, keeping the wooded area on your left. The lake is lost to view behind this wooded area and you walk some way before the lake suddenly appears once more on your left. Hosts of water birds occupy this stretch of water, including swans, moorhens and coots. Follow the lake all the way round until you come to a large bridge with iron railings. Just across from you are the remains of a quite impressive temple, but unfortunately they are within private grounds and you will not be able to get much closer than you are now.

5. At the bridge, turn right and follow the well-marked track along through the woods. Soon you will come onto the golf course again. Keep the course on your left and walk on down the slight hill. Pass through a kissing gate and onto a metalled road. Turn right on this road, following it back over the River Frome and past the creamery. Return over the stile, through the grounds of Oldford Farm, and back to where you left your car.